"What a difference meeting Mike Brooks and reading his two books, The Ultimate Book of Phone Scripts *and* Power Phone Scripts, *have made in my agency's productivity. We have experienced double-digit sales increases in a short period of time!* Power Phone Scripts *expands on the concepts developed in the first book,* The Ultimate Book of Phone Scripts. *It provides an in-depth collection of all the scripts and phone techniques necessary to turn your sales results around. Thank you, Mike, for writing these invaluable books, which are a must read for my team and the focus of many of our meetings. You have challenged me to live by your mantra: 'If they can do it, I can do it better.'"*

—Bruce Adorian, State Farm agent

"If you use the phone to make your sales calls, this book is a must-have! *Mike offers his secrets to better calling to help you make more money—faster!"*

—Michael Krause author of *SMART Prospecting That Works Every Time*

"A sign of wisdom is the ability to learn from your mistakes and successes, and also to learn from the mistakes and successes of others. Mike Brooks is no sales theorist. He's been in the trenches and has risen from struggling salesperson to one of the top salespeople and sales trainers in the world today. His success is evidence of the fact that when you're committed to studying the fundamentals of something and applying what you've learned on a consistent basis, your success is inevitable. Mike's Power Phone Scripts *provides a road map to your sales success. Success is the result of small activities repeated over time. Don't read this book: study it. Apply what you learn, and you too will be able to chart your own sales success regardless of industry, product, or service. Thanks for your sales wisdom, Mike!"*

—Kevin Knebl, CMEC, social selling and relationship marketing specialist and CEO of Knebl Communications, LLC

"Preparation is the key to success in sales. Stop winging it! Prepare yourself to excel with Mike Brooks's proven, practical scripts and make more sales."

—Tom Hopkins, author of *How to Master the Art of Selling* and *When Buyers Say No*

"I have been reading and following Mike Brooks now for over a decade, and I can honestly say that he is the master of inside sales. When I reviewed Mike's new book, Power Phone Scripts, *I was struck once again by how easy he makes it to handle any selling situation—no matter how complex. His scripts are simple, step-by-step responses that work. In this new volume of scripts, Mike goes even deeper by giving us the "Ten Characteristics of Top Sales Producers." You will discover how, by following these principles, you can be and create top producers, too. If you need results from your inside sales team (or you are the team!), then get this book today!"*

—Laura Posey, chief instigator, Simple Success Plans

POWER PHONE SCRIPTS

POWER PHONE SCRIPTS

500 WORD-FOR-WORD QUESTIONS, PHRASES, AND CONVERSATIONS TO OPEN AND CLOSE MORE SALES

MIKE BROOKS

MR. INSIDE SALES

WILEY

Published by John Wiley & Sons, Inc., Hoboken, New Jersey.
Published simultaneously in Canada.

For general information about our other products and services, please contact our Customer Care Department within the United States at (800) 762-2974, outside the United States at (317) 572-3993, or fax (317) 572-4002.

Wiley publishes in a variety of print and electronic formats and by print-on-demand. Some material included with standard print versions of this book may not be included in e-books or in print-on-demand. If this book refers to media such as a CD or DVD that is not included in the version you purchased, you may download this material at http://booksupport.wiley.com. For more information about Wiley products, visit www.wiley.com.

Library of Congress Cataloging-in-Publication Data:

Names: Brooks, Mike, 1957- author.
Title: Power phone scripts : 500 word-for-word questions, phrases, and
   conversations to open and close more sales / Mike Brooks.
Description: Hoboken, New Jersey : John Wiley & Sons, Inc., [2017] | Includes
   bibliographical references and index. |
Identifiers: LCCN 2017013703 (print) | LCCN 2017021433 (ebook) | ISBN
   9781119417958 (pdf) | ISBN 9781119417972 (epub) | ISBN 9781119418078
   (cloth)
Subjects: LCSH: Telephone selling.
Classification: LCC HF5438.3 (ebook) | LCC HF5438.3 .B75 2017 (print) | DDC
   658.8/72—dc23
LC record available at https://lccn.loc.gov/2017013703

Cover Design: Wiley
Cover Image: © Pranch/Shutterstock

Printed in the United States of America.

10 9 8 7 6 5 4 3 2 1

This book is dedicated to you, my fellow sales professional. I believe in you, and if you can believe in yourself, then I guarantee you can achieve an amazing life through learning how to sell more, with less resistance, using the scripts and strategies you will find in this book. You and your family deserve it.

Contents

FOREWORD

L et me be brutally honest. The telephone is, has always been, and will continue to be your most powerful sales tool. Not email. Not social media. The phone!

The brutal and undeniable truth is that inside sales reps who fail to master the phone fail, so it's time to stop looking at the phone like it's your enemy and see it for what it really is: a money-making machine.

The telephone is more effective than email and social media because when you are actually speaking to another human being, there is a higher probability that you'll set appointments, gather qualifying information, and close deals.

Yet, many salespeople find it awkward to use the phone because they:

- Don't know what to say or how to say it.

- Wing it on every call and say stupid, embarrassing things that generate resistance and rejection.

- Don't have easy-to-execute telephone scripts that allow them to focus on their prospect rather than what to say.

- Don't have effective strategies for dealing with reflex responses, brush-offs, and objections.

What I find across the board, though, is that most salespeople don't know how to use the phone for sales because they've never been taught.

This problem is exacerbated by the fact that at most companies, there is deficient to nonexistent telephone training. When companies do provide training, it is usually made up of complex, contrived methods developed by people who've never even successfully used the phone for sales. This approach never works in the real world with real prospects.

Sadly, most salespeople are making egregious mistakes on the phone. Through their words and approach, they turn prospects off, get shut down, and create resistance where it didn't exist.

In inside sales, you have mere seconds to get your prospect's attention. When you have a prospect on the phone, message matters. What you say and how you say it is often the difference between winning or losing the deal.

This is where Mike Brooks comes in. Mike isn't a theorist. He's a trench warrior. He's walked in your shoes. Made the same mistakes, lived through the same pain, and dealt with rejection.

He's also been phenomenally successful. Mike's formula for inside sales excellence was developed through trial and error—working with real prospects, in real time, in the real world. It was honed in the trenches, and it works!

In this book, *Power Phone Scripts: 500 Word-for-Word Questions, Phrases, and Conversations to Open and Close More Sales*, Mike teaches you exactly what to say, when to say it, and how to say it. You'll learn the keys to getting past resistance, dealing with objections, and closing the deal. When you follow Mike's formula, you are guaranteed to improve your performance, boost your income, and attain the success you desire.

Jeb Blount, author of the number-one bestseller
Fanatical Prospecting and CEO of SalesGravy.com

INTRODUCTION

Dear Fellow Sales Professional:

I want this book to be the most important book you will ever read in your sales career.

Actually, I want you to look back at this and someday say that this was the most important book you've ever read in your life. I know that is a strong statement, but let me tell you why. Years ago, I was introduced to a sales philosophy and given a set of tools and techniques that changed all my sales results, and literally changed my life. I went from a struggling salesperson who hated his job, hated prospecting for business, and hated rejection, to a success. I went from driving a beat-up Nissan hatchback to driving a new Mercedes Benz. I went from struggling to pay my credit cards each month to buying my first home and furnishing it just the way I wanted it. I went from dreading waking up every morning to waking up with an enthusiasm and confidence I had never known was possible. And it was all from learning and practicing the habits and techniques I am going to teach you in this book today.

Please don't think I'm bragging, because I am not. Instead, I like what Anthony Robbins said once: "I am not telling you these things to impress you, but rather to impress upon you." What I'm trying to impress upon you today is that if I—a failing and resentful sales rep who thought that life should have dealt him a better card (I was too good to be cold calling as an inside sales rep! I should be doing something more interesting and prestigious with my college degree. . . .)—could turn my attitude, my results, and my life completely around to having the kind of freedom and success I never thought possible, that if I could do all that using the skills, philosophy, and scripts contained in this book, *you* can do it too.

In fact, I guarantee that if you will just follow the advice you will read in this book, you, too, can completely change your sales results.

No matter how poorly (or how well) you are doing now, you can immediately begin doing better. You can begin prospecting with confidence and even get to a place where it becomes fun. Imagine that! By using the scripts and techniques in this book, you can also begin closing more sales and handling objections and stalls—that may frustrate you now—with ease. And as you learn these powerful and proven techniques, you will not only grow more confident, but you will begin to stand out in your company and in your industry. Soon, you will find yourself in the top elite of producers—the "Top 20 Percent," as I like to call them.

As you begin to change your sales results, your life will change as well. Not only will you begin elevating your lifestyle, but your future will begin to change, also. You will begin thinking about things you may not be considering now, like perhaps moving into management or becoming a director of sales or VP of sales. Some of you will begin thinking of opening your own company and using the strategies you will learn here to build a highly successful inside sales team of your own. As you become more successful using these techniques, your world will open up for you, and the sky will become the limit.

As you do all this, you will be changing your family's lives as well. Suddenly you will be able to afford a better house, better cars, and all the stuff you may wish you had now.

Your kids will be able to go to better schools because you will have the resources to afford them. You and your spouse will begin vacationing in the spots and staying in the hotels you always dreamed of staying in, if that's important to you. You will begin saving more money for retirement, and putting money into other savings and investments. You will begin living with a sense of security that you may only dream of now, because you will no longer have financial insecurity. You will be able to sleep better at night because you will finally possess the key to selling well.

All these things and more are available to you once you read and make a commitment to learning and using the strategies, scripts, and techniques you'll find in this book. Again, I know this to be true because it happened for me. Not only that, but since I figured out the secret to selling easily and with less rejection, I have also taught it to hundreds of companies and thousands of sales reps. Have they all had the results I'm promising you here? Sadly, no. Unfortunately, many sales reps were too lazy to put in the relatively brief amount of time necessary (about 90 days of committed effort) to change the way they were doing things. Instead, they continued to ad-lib their way through their sales calls, and simply relied on their old habits. As a result, as they say, "if nothing changes, nothing changes." And nothing did for them.

However, there have been hundreds of sales professionals who were ready for a better life and were willing to make the commitment, put in the effort, and follow the advice detailed in this book. They, without fail, have achieved a higher level of success and the ease and comfort that come from mastering these proven sales strategies and techniques. And, yes, many of them have gone on to be in the Top 20 Percent, and even the Top 1 Percent of the sales professionals in their respective industries. And *you* can, too.

I developed a mantra when I was learning these techniques all those years ago, a mantra I used to say to myself to keep me practicing and to keep me committed to changing my results. I invite you to adopt it as well. As I sat at my desk in the sea of sales reps, I would look around at the top three producers at my company (out of 25 sales reps—many struggling like me), and I thought about the results they consistently produced. They were always on top of the revenue production each month, and they were the ones who drove the nice cars, wore the nice suits, and won all the bonuses. I remember thinking that they had the same amount of hours in a day as I did. They had access to the same scripts and leads. They were selling the same product I was. That is when I developed this mantra:

"If they can do it, I can do it better!"

I was convinced that if they could do it—heck, they were just as human as I was—then I could do it better. I burned with a desire to change my life. I was sick and tired of struggling, and I knew that if they could achieve the results I wanted, then I could and would dedicate myself to learning better techniques and to critiquing myself and my approach daily (through listening to my recordings), and I would invest the time, money, and energy needed to become a top producer.

I did. By relentlessly studying, learning, and applying the strategies (especially the "Ten Characteristics of Top Sales Producers") you will read in this book, and by memorizing, drilling, rehearsing, and adapting the word-for-word scripts you will find here, within 90 days I became one of the top three producers in my company. I still remember the incredible feeling I had when I went up before all 25 reps to accept my award for being a top producer. I still remember my commitment to myself as I walked back to my chair: "And you just wait until next month," I said under my breath as I took my seat.

Nine months later, by continuing to practice and improve, I was the top producer out of five branch offices in Southern California. That next year the company elevated me to the sales manager of the other 25 sales reps in our office. Within one year, I had doubled our office's production by carefully teaching and coaching adherence to the proven principles you'll read in this book. Most sales reps I worked with immediately increased their sales, and many even moved into the Top 20 Percent. Without fail, everyone I have worked with over the years since sees improvement in direct proportion to their commitment level and their adherence to the principles and scripts in this book.

WHY YOU NEED PHONE SCRIPTS

As far as "phone scripts" go, let's address the raging debate about whether inside sales reps should use scripts or not. Everyone has an opinion on this, and while some may be on the fence about it, most people are either very against using a scripted approach, while others advocate using scripts and spend a lot of time and effort creating them for their teams. *Those who don't believe in using them cite many reasons, including*:

- Using scripts makes you sound like a telemarketer.
- Following a script is too confining—you have to be able to "go with the flow" of a conversation.
- You can't consult with a prospect if you're following a script.
- Scripts all sound so "sales-y" that it turns prospects off.

- People can always tell that you're reading something, so you sound unprofessional.

- You can't script out everything—sometimes you just need to be able to ad-lib a little.

- Scripts were okay in the beginning or as a guide, but now that you're a "pro," you don't need them.

And so on. I bet you can think of a few reasons yourself why you'd never be caught dead following a script.

Then there are those who believe that you absolutely must follow a script. Having written several books on phone scripts, you can imagine I subscribe to this group. *Some of the reasons I believe you should follow a script are:*

- Following a script actually makes you sound *more* professional.

- Using a carefully constructed script allows you to follow best-practice sales techniques that have been proven to work over time.

- Following a script ensures that you ask all the right qualifying questions.

- Scripts make your job easier because you know where you've been and where you're going.

- Scripts allow you to truly *listen* to what your prospect is really saying.

- Having a script to follow gives you confidence and control over the sales process.

- Following a scripted sales approach allows you to practice perfection on every call.

Each of these reasons for following a scripted sales approach powerfully affects each stage of your sales process, and any one of them can make or break a sale. The real argument I present to those who insist on not using scripts is this: whether you know it or not, you already *are* following a script!

Think about it: If I were to record all your calls for a week and then transcribe them and hand that transcription back to you, isn't it true that what I would be giving you was your own "script"? Isn't it true that you are saying the same things, over and over again, each time you get a question, objection, or blow-off? Sure you are!

You see, right now everyone is already using a script of some kind, but the problem with most of them is that they were developed in the heat of the sale, on the fly, while they were taking "incoming" from a prospect or client. Most of the responses sales reps use were thought up on the spot and in response to (and often in defense to) some type of difficult sales situation.

Just think about how you, or your sales team, habitually respond to blow-offs like, "What is this call in regard to?" or "We wouldn't be interested," or "Just email me something." Chances are, you are using the same old ineffective responses that just cause you frustration and phone reluctance.

One of the biggest benefits to using professionally prepared scripts, however, is that you can design the most effective response *in advance*, and then deliver your lines like a professional. I often like to cite Marlon Perkins from the old TV show, "Mutual of Omaha's Wild Kingdom," when making this point.

As some of you may remember, his associate, Jim, was always out in the field "wrestling with the alligators," while Marlon was reporting from the "safety and comfort of the Land Rover." I always remember Marlon taking a sip of iced tea and thinking, "When I grow up, I want to be Marlon and not Jim."

In sales, it's the same thing. If you are not following a prepared and effective approach, then each time your prospect answers, you are suddenly like Jim, "wrestling with the alligators." If you take the time, however, in the safety and comfort of the conference room, to craft out the best responses, statements, and questions to the selling situations you run into day after day, then you can calmly and coolly deal with all those situations successfully. And even take a sip of iced tea in between responses!

Here is *one of the most important things to remember* about sales: 80 percent of the brush-offs, the objections and the selling situations you get, day in and day out, are exactly the same. There is very little new in sales. Three thousand years ago in the open markets in Egypt, when a seller told a buyer the price of something, the buyer probably said, "The price is too high!" Sound familiar? Eighty percent of the selling situations you face today are the same ones you faced yesterday, last month, and they are the same ones you will get next week and next summer.

I cannot stress enough how important this concept is in sales. It gives you, the sales professional, a *huge* advantage *if* you take the time to capitalize on it. Unfortunately, the majority of sales reps and companies never leverage this fact, but the Top 20 Percent of sales producers do take advantage of this by taking the time to script out proven and effective responses to these objections so they are prepared in advance to succeed. Then, when they get the same old objections or stalls, they know exactly how to handle them. They understand the importance of taking the time to drill, practice, and rehearse effective responses so they can deliver their scripts in a natural and professional tone and at an optimal pace. That is why top producers sound so smooth and professional, and why they make sales seem easy. Because they have taken the time to internalize their best-practice scripts, top performers deliver their responses naturally, and they automatically know exactly what to say and when to say it.

And just a word about practice. Did you notice I didn't say they "read their scripts"? Every professional—whether an actor, musician, dancer, or athlete—spends hours and hours learning their craft and practicing their techniques so that when it's time to perform, they do it automatically. All those concerts you see performed by large orchestras and dance routines that seem easy and effortless are all the results of hundreds of hours of careful practice. Don Shula, the Super Bowl–winning coach of the Miami Dolphins, talks about how his players practice every day until their assignments and techniques become automatic. He said, "Overlearning means that the players are so prepared for a game that they have the skill and confidence needed to make the big play."

It is the same with any sales professional. If you need to think about how to respond to a question, a blow-off, an objection, or a stall, then it's already too late. If you have scripted out the best approach or response and memorized it, however, then you will have the skill and confidence to handle those situations like a top producer. This is what empowers you to be successful, and it is what separates you from the other 80 percent who are struggling and making things up as they go along.

So, should you learn and use best-practice, real-world responses that give you the greatest chance to succeed in the selling situations you get into day after day? Or should you continue to make things up as you go along, hoping that what you say will occasionally work? The answer to that question will determine whether or not you choose to learn and use scripts, and how successful—or unsuccessful—you will be in your career.

Speaking of scripts, if you have not yet read, practiced, and perfected the core inside sales scripts in my original, bestselling book *The Ultimate Book of Phone Scripts*, you will benefit even more from those essential scripts. In *The Ultimate Book of Phone Scripts*, you will find over 200 scripts that give you and your sales team proven and effective ways to easily deal with gatekeepers, get through to more decision makers, overcome objections, and close more sales. *The Ultimate Book of Phone Scripts* lays the groundwork for selling over the phone and provides the fundamental scripts you need to be successful. Combined with the advanced and additional scripts and strategies you will find here in *Power Phone Scripts*, you and your sales team will have *all* the scripts and phone techniques you will ever need to completely turn your sales results around and transform your career, your life, and your company. Get *The Ultimate Book of Phone Scripts* here: http://mrinsidesales.com/ultimatescripts.htm.

One last word about investing in yourself, your company, and your success. If you are a business owner or sales manager and you want the quickest lift from an investment in your sales team, then do this: buy each member of your sales team a copy of both *Ultimate Book*s, and task them with studying, adapting, and incorporating these proven scripts into their sales presentations. Have your sales manager conduct sales meetings to teach these proven scripts and concepts, and watch your sales and revenues begin to take off.

This is the most important thing you can do to improve the sales results in your company, because the number one reason the majority of all sales teams struggle is that not many managers are experienced or prepared enough to gives sales reps—the ones in the trenches—the word-for-word scripts and tools they need to succeed. Very few companies are effectively or consistently teaching sales reps what to say and do when they are faced with an objection or challenging sales situation. If you doubt this, then hold a sales meeting and go around the room asking each rep how they handle the standard sales stall of, "I need to ask my partner." I will bet you right now that each rep will ad-lib a different (and mostly ineffective) answer. This is why your sales team is struggling. The only way to fix that—and so fix your sales results—is to finally give them the exact scripts they need to deal effectively with this and the other selling objections and situations they run into day after day. If you don't do this, then your team will continue to struggle and produce inconsistent results—it's as simple as that. If you do address this glaring need, then your team will immediately begin producing more sales and you will finally have a way to scale a successful inside sales team—and company.

If you are a sales professional working at a company and you're struggling with the idea of investing another $39.95 in a book of phone scripts, ask yourself how much money you paid for all those college textbooks that you sold back to the student store for a quarter of their value? You know, the ones you can't remember anything about right now. Then compare all those hundreds of dollars you spent (and are still probably paying for through your outstanding student loans), to the under-$100 total investment in these two books of *Ultimate Phone Scripts* and *Power Phone Scripts* that will make your every phone call better and which will dramatically improve your life for years to come. It is a no-brainer when you look at it this way. If you put just 90 days into studying and applying the proven techniques and scripts you will find in these two books, you will transform your life. So go ahead, make the investment in yourself, and start changing your future today.

HOW TO GET THE MOST FROM THIS BOOK

The book is broken down into three parts: Part One: Laying the Groundwork for Success; Part Two: Prospecting Techniques and

Scripts; and Part Three: Closing Techniques and Scripts. I suggest you start with Part One, and the Ten Characteristics of Top Sales Producers, to see how many of these you are practicing now and how many you can begin incorporating into your sales life. Each of these core characteristics are practiced by top sales producers across all industries, and even incorporating just one a week can cause a huge shift in your perspective and in your sales results. One of my go-to techniques, for example, is recording and critiquing yourself every day for 90 days.

You have probably heard of this suggestion of recording yourself, and your company may regularly record your calls now, but how often do you take it upon yourself to review your own calls? Just this one technique will have a dramatic and instant impact on how you sell, and I personally doubled my income in 90 days by applying this technique in my own career. Every other characteristic will also add to your success, so study and apply each characteristic starting today.

Next, in Part Two: Prospecting Techniques and Scripts, you will find current and proven scripts to help you cold-call prospects and qualify better prospects. You'll find many current and proven rebuttals to the blow-offs you may be encountering now (things like, "I'm not interested," and "I'm too busy," and so on). You'll also find ways to qualify in crucial, core areas like budget, interest, and competition. Remember that you can't close an unqualified lead, so learning how to carefully qualify a prospect (without interrogating them) will immediately take your sales skills—and closing results—to another level. As with all these scripts, make sure to invest the time to adapt them to your product, service, and personality. Make them your own and then commit to memorizing them and using them until they become automatic for you. This is how you will develop the habits of a Top 20 Percent producer.

In Part Three: Closing Techniques and Scripts, you will finally learn some advanced skills to help you handle a variety of situations that may frustrate you today. Among the techniques you will learn is how to use tie-downs to build a yes momentum. This is important, because in today's sale, the game isn't about pitching and pitching and then ending with a grand close or prayer that someone buys. The game is, instead, about presenting your product or services gradually and getting buy-in from your prospect so you know how the sale is going. As you successfully get that buy-in, asking for the sale becomes a natural part of the overall sales process. By the time you do, you should have a good idea of what the result will be—and how to handle it.

There are also many word-for-word scripts to help you deal with the objections and stalls you may be struggling with now. You will find proven ways to handle things like, "I want to think about it," and "The price is too high," and "We're happy with who we're using now." Once again, your task here is to carefully study these word-for-word scripts, adapt them to your product, service, and personality, and then practice, drill, and rehearse them until they become your new and improved way of automatically reacting and presenting. If you do this, you will begin closing more sales with less rejection.

You will also read about a way to stand out from your competition and position yourself to be the go-to vendor or solution just when your prospect is in the market (page 248). It is called "Send Out Cards" (https://www.sendoutcards.com/mrinsidesales). This completely automated service allows you to send customized greeting cards (and even gifts) to prospects and customers with the click of a button. The real power, however, is your ability to set up an automatic drip campaign that will send any prospect in your pipeline cards at any interval you choose. This system has made me hundreds of thousands of dollars in business that seems to have appeared out of the air. In reality, people are just reaching out to me when they finally need help—motivated to do so by monthly cards they receive. In this way, I'm able to stay "top of mind," and they remember to reach out to me when they suddenly decide to do something about their inside sales training needs. Using the link mentioned here, you learn more about this valuable service, and even can try it out by sending a free card to yourself—I encourage you to do this today.

Finally, a last note to you, my fellow sales producer. Remember, you *can* become a top producer if you are willing to put in the time to learn and then practice the techniques you will find in this book. I want to encourage you with all of my heart. I guarantee that you and your family will have an infinitely better life if you just commit yourself to the strategies, scripts, and techniques you'll read in this book. Look around at the top producers sitting next to you or in your industry and say to yourself: "If they can do it, I can do it better."

And you can.

PART I

LAYING THE GROUNDWORK FOR SUCCESS

CHAPTER **1**

What It Takes to Be a Top Producer

Ten Characteristics of Top Sales Producers

If you are reading this book right now, then I know you want to perform better in your sales career. If you are a business owner, then I know you want to help your sales team accomplish more. It shows that you are willing to take the time to search out strategies and learn the word-for-word scripts that will give you an edge over your competition. That's a good thing, but are you ready to really commit to doing the things that will catapult you into that rarified stratum of top sales producers?

You know the top producers I am talking about. They are the ones who are always at or near the top of the sales production list every month, who always win the sales contests, and who always seem to be in a good mood. They are positive and confident, and they have that feeling that no matter what happens to the leads or the economy or the company, they will find a way to succeed.

Years ago I heard a sales motivator say:

> "If you are willing to do the things that most sales reps aren't willing to do, then soon you'll be able to do and have the things that most sales reps will never be able to do and have."

When I heard that statement, I was a struggling sales rep, and I was sick and tired of being sick and tired. I was at a crossroads in my career (and my life), and I was either going to find a different way of making a living, or I was going to go back to school and get out of sales altogether.

What I did was commit to being one of the top producers.

I heard another motivator say that if the grass looks greener on the other side of the street, then you need to fertilize your lawn. He said that you don't have to change where you are in order to succeed, but rather that you can bloom where you are planted.

And as I mentioned before, I had many examples of that in the company where I worked. The top producers made it look easy. They never seemed to struggle. They instead seemed to intuitively know how to handle almost any sales situation. It was inspiring and intimidating at the same time. It wasn't until I finally made a commitment to be one of them that I saw how much time, discipline, and effort they put into being the best.

While it did take a lot of effort for me to get there from where I was as a struggling sales rep, with commitment, determination, and daily focus, it was all worth it. Once I became a top producer, I felt like I knew the secret of what it took to live a better life, to enjoy the job and profession that just 90 days before I hated. Suddenly, I understood how easy it was—once I was ready to do the things it took to be a top producer.

And you can do it, too.

The good news, as I have said, is that success leaves clues, and if you are willing to invest the time, money, and effort into completely changing your results and your life, then you can. You *can* bloom where you are planted, and you can start enjoying the things that top producers take for granted—the things that most sales reps will never get to enjoy.

You will find what I consider to be the top ten characteristics of top sales producers. These are not only the things I did to completely change my results and reach the top, but they are also the things I see in nearly every top producer, in every company, that I have coached and consulted with over the past 25 years.

As you read through the list, look at the top producers at your company (you may even be one of the top reps already), and ask yourself how many of them are doing these things. Look at your own behavior and ask yourself how many of these things *you* are doing, and how many of them you can begin practicing right now.

I guarantee that the more of these characteristics you adopt, the more successful you will be.

So if you're ready, then let's get started.

TOP CHARACTERISTIC #1: MAKE A COMMITMENT

Let me ask you this: Are you willing to make an intensive, 90-day commitment to transforming your sales career? Would you be willing if I told you that by diligently following the proven techniques and scripts you will learn in this book, you would make a dramatic improvement in how you prospect and qualify new business, how you conduct your sales presentation, and how you deal with objections and close business? If I told you that you could move into the Top 20 Percent of the producers in your company and even double your income in just 90 days, would you be willing to make the commitment to do what is necessary?

If your answer is yes, then get ready to radically change many of your habits, and get ready to put in the time it's going to take to completely change the way you sell over the phone. As you will continue to read in this section of 10 characteristics, there are many things you are going to be doing differently, but if you make the commitment now to adopting and incorporating these techniques into your selling career, then the results can and will be life changing. But it is all going to start with making that commitment.

The best way to think about this is like making a commitment to getting an A in a college course that is run on the quarter system. If any of you have attended a quarter course in college before, then you know how much is packed into each weekly session. I remember that on the first day of class at UCLA, the instructor went through the first three chapters of the textbook. By the end of the one-and-a-half-hour class, I was already behind three chapters. And that was one of only five classes I was taking that quarter! What I had to do was seriously commit to studying, drilling, and rehearsing the material over and over again. With a lot of hard work and effort, I did ace the class, but it took a total commitment at the very beginning.

The same thing will be true for you in learning a new set of skills, habits, and techniques to help you sell over the phone. In fact, one of the most difficult things you will have to do is to "unlearn" the way you do things now. Right now, you probably do things automatically—and incorrectly. Learning a new way of responding to the objections you get over and over again will be a challenge, and you'll have to practice, drill, rehearse, and record yourself relentlessly to change those old habits, but once you do, something magical happens.

Once you start diligently working to change, improve, and adopt new ways of qualifying, dealing with stalls, and closing sales, your results begin to dramatically change. Suddenly, situations that used to frustrate you begin to get easier to handle, and soon you find yourself winning more and more sales. As you do, your confidence goes up, and so does your paycheck! At the end of each month, there is actually money left over, and suddenly you can begin saving for and buying the things that matter to you and your family. No more struggling because you don't have enough money. How will that feel?

All of this begins affecting you differently outside of the office as well. Suddenly, you begin sleeping better, no longer worrying about money and bills. You wake up with a new energy (rather than dread), and Mondays are positively transformed! Your spouse and kids begin noticing a difference, and you soon start seeing the world as a place of opportunity rather than one of closed-ended traps. Literally, your world changes. You can achieve all this if you are simply willing to make that 90-day commitment to get started.

In addition to the immediate changes, though, what making the commitment also does for you is alter the future of your career. That's because once you learn proven and effective skills for selling over the phone, your results change not only for the next 90 days, but for the rest of this year, and all the ones that follow. As soon as you adopt a new, successful way of selling, everything becomes easier for you. New opportunities in management open up, your career path changes, and your confidence and enthusiasm for the profession of sales completely transforms. All of a sudden, sales becomes the greatest of professions, and your choices of what to sell, and where, are unlimited. And all you have to do is make a commitment today to putting in the time and effort required to get there.

For everything you will gain, 90 days of intense study and practice are well worth the effort. In essence, all you are doing is developing new habits that will become your new, automatic way of doing things. I heard a saying years ago that I still repeat today:

"First we form habits, and then they form us."

Once you form your new, more effective selling habits, they will transform you into a top producer at your company, and in your industry. Once again, I know because it happened for me. I still fondly look back on the 90 days I took to script out and memorize more effective responses. I still remember sitting in the conference room at lunchtime listening to my recordings with a buddy and critiquing each other's calls. I remember the determination I had as I got back on the phone that afternoon—determined not to make the same mistakes, to mute myself and listen to what my prospect was telling me.

Most of all, I remembered what that sales trainer told us the month before: "if you are willing to do the things that most sales reps aren't willing to do, then you will soon be able to have and enjoy the things that most sales reps will never be able to have." Soon I was driving a better car, buying my first house, and winning the trip to Hawaii at the end of the year. I still remember the feeling I had being picked up in a limousine (paid for by the company) in Maui and driven along the coastline to my hotel on the beach. I can't tell you how grateful I am that I was willing to make that commitment to myself!

So if you are willing to make that commitment to have a better sales career and life, then read on and get ready to make the changes that will have an enduring effect on everything you do from here on out.

TOP CHARACTERISTIC #2: BE PREPARED FOR RECURRING SELLING SITUATIONS

This is absolutely huge. The strange thing is that 80 percent of sales-people (and sales teams) simply don't take the time or make the effort to do it. Now that you have made the commitment, this one tip will catapult your sales and your confidence.

Remember what I said earlier: one of the most important things you will ever learn about sales is that 80 to 90 percent of the objections, stalls, put-offs, and sales situations you run into day after day are the same. The blow-offs you got yesterday are the same ones you got last month and that you'll get next month and next year. Think about it: How many times do you hear this when you prospect or cold call?

From the gatekeeper:

"Will he know what this call is regarding?"

From the prospect:

"I wouldn't be interested."

"We already have someone who handles that."

"Just email me something."

Do any of these sound familiar? Of course they do! And I will bet you could add another four or five, couldn't you?

And how about the objections and stalls you get when you close a sale? How about these:

"We just aren't ready to make a decision yet."

"I'm going to have to talk to my partner/boss/spouse/committee."

"Your price isn't in our budget."

Are these sounding familiar? Of course they are! Once again, you could easily come up with about five or seven more, couldn't you?

Again, here is the point: the best thing about sales—and what makes it so easy for top performers who recognize and prepare for it—is that there are only about seven or nine objections or stalls per selling situation, per product, or service. You keep getting them over and over and over again!

Now here is the problem: most sales reps and companies do not leverage this important fact. Knowing what the objections and stalls are in advance is like knowing all the answers to an exam ahead of time. If you knew what the answers for a final exam were going to be, wouldn't you script out the correct answers in advance? Of course you would! Yet for some unknown reason, most sales reps don't take the time to script out and then practice, drill, and rehearse the most effective responses ahead of time. Instead, 80 percent of sales reps (and sales teams) choose to ad-lib and make up ineffective responses to these repeatable selling situations, stalls, or objections. This dooms them to fail and is perhaps the biggest problem in the selling profession today. It makes most sales reps' lives a living nightmare, and it is why most inside sales teams fail to reach their revenue goals.

Top producers, on the other hand, do leverage this sales fact to stack the odds in their favor.

They take the time to develop, memorize, and then deliver effective responses to these objections, and so they easily handle and overcome them. They are not afraid of getting resistance. They are instead prepared for it. Knowing what is coming and being prepared for it enables them to listen to what their prospect is saying and allows them to question the objection and find out what is really holding a prospect back. This makes them confident and allows them to stay in the game and overcome the stalls and objections while other sales reps fold and go away. This allows top producers to persevere and close more sales. It also makes their job easy and stress-free, because they know in advance what's coming, and they are prepared for it.

An example would be the objection: "I'm going to need to check with the boss." Eighty percent of sales reps handle this common smokescreen objection incorrectly by saying something like: "Well, when should I call you back?"

By doing it this way, they simply create a stall and then they worry that when they finally do hear back from the prospect, the answer will be, "Well, the boss doesn't want to do it."

How many times has this happened to you?

A top producer, on the other hand, handles this very differently. Instead, because she has prepared for this recurring smokescreen in advance, she knows two or three proven ways to get around it. So instead of creating a stall, she uses a script that gets her prospect to reveal the true objection. She would say:

> "I understand and I'm curious about something. Let's say for a moment that your boss can go either way on this and tells you to do whatever you think is best, based on what we've gone over so far and what you understand about this. What would you likely do?"

This is called isolating the smokescreen objection, and based on what the prospect then says, the top producer will have the information she needs to take the next effective step. Hint: Any answer other than, "I would do it" means that talking to the so-called boss is a smokescreen and *not* the real objection. If this is the case, then the producer has more work to do to uncover what is really holding this prospect back. And guess how she's going to do that? By using additional scripts that she has prepared in advance.

This is what I mean by knowing what is coming in advance, and then being able to leverage that knowledge and effectively and competently handle it.

And that is your assignment for this week. Start by making a list of all the stalls, put-offs, and objections you get with your sale during the prospecting call, the presentation, and all the follow-up calls. Then commit to adapting and customizing the many scripts you'll read in this book so they are just right to handle them. Then, once you've found the ones that work (I recommend you script out three or four responses for each objection), spend the time to practice, drill, and rehearse those best-practice responses until you can deliver each one automatically.

If you are willing to do this—again, what 80 percent of your competition won't take the time and effort to do—then soon you will enjoy closing more sales, making more money, and living a more confident and successful life as a sales professional.

TOP CHARACTERISTIC #3: RECORD & CRITIQUE YOUR CALLS FOR 90 DAYS

A top inside sales trainer, Stan Billue, first introduced me to this concept. He said that nothing would help you double your income in 90 days faster than recording and critiquing your calls each day. He also said that most sales reps would not be willing to do this (and he's right). But, he said, if you *are* willing to do it, then you can quickly move into the Top 20 Percent of the selling professionals in your company and industry. (He was right there, too.)

If you have any resistance to this idea, then just remember that all professionals record their performances and use them to improve how they practice and perform. Think about how much time football players spend watching game film, or dancers spend watching film of their practices and performances, or actors and directors spend watching a previous day's shoot.

Every professional records, critiques, and gets better by analyzing and improving their technique, their strategies, and their performance by recording and breaking down each part of their performance. You need to, as well. Once I made a commitment to recording and carefully critiquing my calls, I was amazed by how much I found. You will be, too. Here are some things to be on the lookout for when playing your calls back.

1. How well did you listen to your prospect or client? This is huge, because once you begin hearing yourself on a sales call, you'll be amazed by how much—and how quickly—you start talking. In fact, you will be stunned by how quickly you start talking over your prospect.

2. Did you hear what your prospect or client was truly saying, or did you just hear what you wanted to hear? Clients

and prospects are always trying to tell us what's important to them, but most of the time, we don't hear it. When you begin listening to your calls, you will see the need to begin using your mute button so you can begin hearing the buying signals—and potential objections.

3. Did you ask all the right qualifying questions? A fundamental problem in sales is that most prospects don't close because they were never properly qualified to begin with. By listening to your recordings and discovering what information you did and didn't get, you'll be able to strengthen your calls on the front end, thereby producing more qualified leads to close later on.

4. Did you follow your best-practice scripts, or did you fall back on your old habits of ad-libbing? In the beginning, you'll find that following a new script is hard! Our tendency is to fall back on our old scripts and start ad-libbing again. By recording yourself, you will begin to hold yourself accountable to the new techniques and scripts you are trying to learn.

5. When answering an objection, did you end by asking for the order, or did you simply talk past the close? This is a common—and huge mistake—because many sales reps are afraid of asking for the order for fear of getting more objections. So when they try to counter an objection, they tend to just keep pitching and describing features and benefits. This leads to more confusion and more questions from the prospect. The proper way to handle an objection is to carefully answer it, confirm your answer, and then ask for the sale again. When listening to your recordings, ask yourself if you are following this proven formula.

6. Did you introduce an objection by talking too much? This will give you shivers the first time you hear yourself doing it.

7. How about tie-downs and trial closes? Most sales reps love to talk. It is a bad habit, because in inside sales, you have

no idea what your prospect is thinking—unless you stop to ask them. By recording yourself, you will get an idea of how much you are talking, and how much you are listening.

8. Are you improving? This is big as well, because we all need positive reinforcement. You need to hear yourself getting better, celebrate your improvement, and see the benefits of all the work you're doing to get better. By recording yourself, you will be able to do just that.

9. How is your tone, your pacing, and your energy? All of these things are crucial on a call, and if you are not objectively listening to yourself, you have no idea of how you sound—and also no way of correcting yourself.

10. You will find many other ways to improve as well—ways that would never occur to you if you were not recording and listening to yourself. It's why the other 80 percent rarely, if ever, improve.

As you begin listening to yourself, you might find that it is uncomfortable in the beginning.

Nobody likes to hear the sound of their own voice, and no one likes to hear how bad they usually are, but don't be put off! Make a commitment to improving on each call every day. I guarantee that if you do, you will soon be happy you did, because nothing pays off faster than practicing this crucial characteristic.

The easiest way to start is to pick a partner at work and begin listening to each other's calls during lunch. Get a buddy, make a commitment to critiquing each other, and be hard on one another in your effort to be better. This is serious work you are doing, and if you are both truly dedicated to improving, you will soon find that it becomes fun—take my word for it! What you will also find is that when you're back on the phone, just before you go off script or talk over someone, you will see your partner's face and you'll hit your mute button to avoid making a mistake that your partner will point out later. This is the way to bring awareness into your selling habits and a way to be mindful on each and every call. It's how you improve dramatically in a short period of time. And remember, the new habits and skills you are developing during this 90-day period will serve you well for months and years to come!

As soon as you can, find a way to record and download your recordings for playback and critique. The sooner you do, the sooner you'll leapfrog over your competition.

TOP CHARACTERISTIC #4: THOROUGHLY QUALIFY EACH PROSPECT

I'll start with a story: I was in the Bay Area conducting onsite training for a group of IT inside sales reps who sold software, and I was talking about what makes up a qualified lead and how important it is. I went over the six things you need to know about each prospect before you set up an appointment or presentation, and then I covered specific scripted questions (along with rebuttals for any resistance) and how to get this information.

The sales reps sat around the conference table with a look of wonder on their faces. Only one person in the back of the room was smiling broadly and nodding his head up and down. It turned out that he was a new rep who had just joined the team after working for IBM. After I was done with the qualifying piece of the training, this rep raised his hand and told the following story:

"I know exactly what you're talking about in terms of fully qualifying leads before setting them up for a demo or appointment. In fact, the number one rep in our division at IBM had a team of 'qualifiers' who would make the initial calls and then turn the leads over to this this guy for his approval.

"This rep (we'll call him Brad), had put together a 'qualifying checklist' of 10 items he demanded his qualifiers ask, and if they turned a lead over without at least eight of the questions answered, he turned the lead back over and told them to call back and get the rest of the questions answered.

"Now here's the thing," this rep said, now almost shaking with enthusiasm. "All the other reps would have been happy if three or four of the questions had been answered. We would all have considered that a good lead to call!

"But not Brad. Brad wouldn't waste his time with what he called 'non-qualified leads,' because he said he didn't need the practice of trying to

close sales. He said he was only interested in pitching and closing qualified leads."

Then he dropped the bomb that made believers out of all the
other sales reps in attendance:

"The thing was, because of this, Brad was the number-one producer in
our division and grossed over $1 million a year in commissions!"

And that is why Characteristic Number 4 is so important. You
need to make sure you are fully qualifying each and every prospect or
lead you generate. I have found from personal experience—and taught
for years—this fundamental truth in sales: you can't close an unqualified lead. You must know the following criteria about every lead before
you set up a demo or appointment:

1. Why will this prospect buy? What are their specific buying
   motives? What are the areas of your pitch that you need to
   concentrate—and get buy-in on—for each prospect? If you
   don't know what each prospect is looking for, then you won't
   know how to speak to it.

2. Why won't this prospect buy? What are the likely roadblocks
   that might stall or derail this sale? Once again, if you don't
   know what you are up against in terms of why the prospect
   might not choose you, then you won't know how to avoid or
   address these key, potentially dangerous areas.

3. Who are all the decision makers? What is this person's role
   in the sales process? If he or she is an influencer, how much
   influence does he or she have, and when in the sales process
   does he or she wield it?

4. Timeline. What is the decision process like? How long will it
   take? How many hoops do you need to jump through? How
   soon—or how long—is your prospect going to take to make
   a decision on this? Knowing this important detail gives you
   leverage over the close and lets you know when—and how
   often—to ask for the sale.

5. Competition. Who are you competing against? Is their
   old supplier or vendor still in the mix? How many other

companies are they looking at? What does your prospect like about your competitor's offer, and why? What is your unique advantage, and how important is it to your prospect? Most of all, why would they choose you over another company or provider?

6. Budget. What is your prospect or client looking to spend for your product or service? Is your solution perceived as having enough value to justify that investment? If not, how can you build that?

These are the six basic qualifiers that you need to know about every lead before you enter the closing area. There may be more given your particular sale, and if so, you'd better create your own qualifying checklist and make sure that you know this information well in advance. (If you would like more detail on how to get this qualifying information, then you will find it in my first book of scripts, *The Ultimate Book of Phone Scripts*, in which I explain this qualification process in detail, along with all the questions you will need at each stage.)

Now, I know we don't live in a perfect world, and not all prospects will sit through a thorough attempt to qualify them. No worries, because if you did not learn everything on the first call, then you can make up for this by "requalifying" at the beginning of your presentation or close. Ask whatever questions you missed during qualifying at the beginning of the presentation call so you will have the leverage you'll need to confidently close later. You will find some specific, scripted ways to do that in the next characteristic.

There is a reason Brad wasn't interested in attempting to close leads that were not completely qualified. He knew the basic rule of sales that I stated earlier: you can't close an unqualified lead. If you are a sales professional or sales manager, just look carefully (and honestly) at your current pipeline, and ask yourself how qualified the prospects in there are. If there are some holes, then requalify them the next time you speak with them. Then, from this point forward, do the right thing from the beginning: fully qualify upfront, and watch your closing ratio—and your income—soar.

TOP CHARACTERISTIC #5: RE-QUALIFY PROSPECTS AT THE BEGINNING OF YOUR CLOSE

To start with, let's see how most sales reps give a closing presentation or demo. Most sales reps get a prospect on the phone, go through a long-winded presentation, and seldom check in. At the end, they vaguely ask for the sale with a weak statement like:

"So, what do you think?"

A client of mine once described his sales team as "spraying and praying." They "sprayed" a long presentation, and then at the end "prayed" the prospect was on board and would buy. If that is how you or your sales team members are doing it now, then you know how sick a feeling it is to finally ask for the sale and get turned down.

Top producers handle this in a very different way. First, top producers put much better quality leads into their sales cylinder because they follow Top Characteristic Number 4 of fully qualifying their leads. Next, when they get a prospect back on the phone, before they jump into their demo or presentation, they take the time up front to requalify their prospect so there are no surprises when they ask for the sale at the end.

What they are requalifying for are things like the decision-making ability of the person they are pitching, the timeline for making the decision (especially using a trial close like: "And if at the end, you like what you see today, is this something you can move forward with?"), and any other qualifying areas that weren't covered during the qualifying call.

Here is a list of some sample questions you can ask at the beginning of your presentation to help requalify your prospect so you have the information you need to guide this call toward a closed sale:

"I know you mentioned last time that you were particularly interested in learning about _____. What other area would you like to see today?"

And

"You mentioned that you were the one who would decide on something like this—is that still the case?"

And

"I know you said you wanted to find a solution as soon as possible, so let me ask you: If this is everything you're looking for, would you be able to make a decision on this today?"

And

"You know, _____, we talked about the range of investment being between $10,000 to $50,000, depending on which program you went with. If you do like this today, what kind of commitment are you thinking of making?"

And

"I'm happy we have some time to go over how all this works, and let me ask you: If after you see the presentation today, you agree this is what you're looking for, is this something you can give me the go-ahead to put to work for you today?"

If some of these questions seem intimidating to you, it is probably because you haven't been thoroughly qualifying your prospects to begin with. You may be more used to the "spray and pray" approach. I am here to tell you that you will close more deals, avoid more frustration, and confidently close more sales if you begin requalifying your prospects up front.

The benefits of doing this are many. To start with, if you find that a prospect isn't going to make a decision at the end of your demo, but rather has lots of concerns or objections already, then you can adjust your pitch accordingly. You can shorten it or ask for their main interest points and address those first. Then, after you have answered any questions, you can begin overcoming some of the obstacles or determining if this is a prospect who is ever going to close at all.

If you find that many of your prospects aren't going to make a decision at the end of your presentation, then you can go back to your qualifying script and put in more specific questions so you get better qualified leads for your next close.

On the other hand, if you find out that your prospect is indeed ready to go, then you can use more tie-downs and trial closes during your presentation to build that important "buying momentum" and then confidently ask for and get the sale sooner. Either way, you will know where you stand at the beginning of your presentation and what you have to do to win the deal.

Take some time this week to restructure the opening of your presentation or demo and put in some of the requalifying questions you read earlier or that you will find later in this book. Or, adapt some of your own. The more you ask these kinds of questions, the stronger a closer you will become.

One last note: don't be afraid that you are going to scare away buyers by doing this.

Buyers will respond to these kinds of questions positively and give you honest answers. Only non-buyers will give you trouble, and wouldn't you rather know up front who is going to buy and who isn't?

TOP CHARACTERISTIC #6: BUILD RAPPORT BEFORE, DURING, AND AFTER A SALE

While most people think that salespeople have the "gift of gab" and can seemingly talk to anybody, it is not that way at all. If you don't believe me, just listen to a few of your own recordings or those of your teammates.

The truth is, knowing how to honestly and naturally build rapport with someone takes a lot of skill, practice, and patience. Unfortunately, most sales reps are in a tremendous hurry to get their pitch out so they often treat prospects as obstacles to go through to get a sale.

This is a big problem.

Years ago, my first sales manager (my older brother, Peter Brooks), taught me an important lesson. As I rushed through a pitch to qualify and then tried to close prospects, he told me that I was missing out on the most important thing—connecting with and treating people with respect and a genuine interest to help them.

He told me, "Michael, these are just people you're speaking with. Treat them as such, and you'll go much further than you are now."

It took awhile for me to relax and overcome my fear of rejection, but as I got more successful, I began to develop a genuine interest in the people I was speaking with. Once I remembered that they had lives, responsibilities, families, fears, and goals just like me, it made talking to them, rather than at them, so much easier.

Once I did that, it was much easier to build real rapport, earn trust, and create an atmosphere that allowed the sale to naturally unfold. You have probably all heard the saying that people buy from people they like, know, and trust, right? When selling over the phone, learning how to develop genuine rapport will help get someone to like, know, and begin to trust you.

You have three opportunities to develop rapport: before (during the initial qualifying call), during (during the close or presentation), and after (once your prospect becomes a client).

Here are some tips on how to build rapport during all three stages.

On the prospecting call. This is perhaps the hardest time to do this, because your prospect doesn't know anything about you other than that you're a sales rep trying to sell them something. This is when their defenses are at their highest.

The way to build rapport during this phase is to concentrate on relating with them right at the beginning, before you start pitching. You do this by asking any number of things like how the weather is ("Is it still over a hundred degrees there?"), or how the new conversion or transition (a project they are involved in) is going, or if they're super busy now that it's Monday, or if they are relieved that it's Friday. Find some common ground and build some rapport around it before you launch into your pitch. Your goal is to try to build a connection before you put your sales hat on.

A good way to do this is to develop a touch-point plan of leaving voice mails and sending emails if you're not able to reach someone right away. By leaving a carefully constructed series of messages beforehand, you can start building that rapport before you even speak with them. Then, when you do reach them, you can begin your conversation by asking if they received your messages and if they have had a chance to read them yet. If not, then build rapport as described before you go into your pitch. (You will get a detailed example of how to build that touch-point plan later in this book.)

Building rapport this way takes a little practice, but if you truly become interested in each and every person you speak with, they will feel it, and you will separate yourself from all the other sales reps who are just trying to sell them. Believe me, this will pay big dividends for you.

Build rapport during your presentation. Most sales reps are in a hurry to get through their pitch so they can see if a prospect is going to buy or not. This is not only bad technique, but it is also rude. Prospects can often detect a sales rep's "commission breath," as one of my clients called it, and nothing turns them off quicker than when they detect yours.

Top producers, on the other hand, continue their interest in their prospect and concentrate on having a conversation throughout their presentation rather than making their pitch a rushed monologue. The way you do this is by putting lots of tie-downs, open-ended questions, and even trial closes into your presentation. Your goal should be to check in with, engage, and involve your prospect in a conversation rather than deliver a pitch.

An example of this is by checking in with your prospect after you have given a benefit or explained how something works. Asking simple things like, "How would that fit in with what you are doing?" or "Does that fit in with your current initiative?" is a good start. Using open-ended questions is good, too. Instead of asking, "Are you with me?" you should ask, "What questions do you have for me so far?" By building rapport in this way, you also begin getting an idea of how interested or engaged your prospect is. The more engaged they are, the better your chances of advancing the sale.

Spend some time this week to rewrite your demo or presentation to give your prospect opportunities to acknowledge, engage, and ask lots of questions. The more rapport you can build during the close, the better.

Continue to build rapport after the sale. Many sales reps are surprised to hear this, but aftercare of a new client is just as important as getting one to begin with. Most sales reps forget a client once their order is complete, but top producers know that right after a prospect has purchased is the best time to either up sell them or get a referral.

The way you do this is by once again having a conversation and expanding upon your rapport. Get in the habit of calling your new clients every week or so just to see how they are doing. Offer any assistance and continue to develop a relationship with them. If you have an opportunity to offer an additional service or product, do so. If not, then have your referral script handy.

Also, consider drip marketing to your new customer by using a greeting card system such as www.sendoutcards.com/mrinsidesales. The more you can "touch" your new client, the stickier they are going to become and the more likely you will be able to do more and longer-term business with them.

In conclusion, building rapport seems to be a lost art for many salespeople. This is why most people (yourself included) hate getting calls from sales reps. Top producers know the value of treating people with respect and with genuine interest. By doing so, you can not only develop a long and loyal customer base, but you can begin to enjoy your career more as well. Sounds like a win-win to me.

Top Characteristic #7: Ask for the Sales Multiple Times

Most sales team's calls I listen to (while reviewing my client's closing and presentation calls), ask for the sale only about one time (if, surprisingly, at all!). If they get a stall or objection, they generally fold and go away in defeat. It's rare that I hear someone ask for the sale more than three times. Think about that for yourself or your sales team. How many times do you ask for the sale before you give up?

I was taught years ago that the close doesn't even *begin* until the prospect has said no at least three times! I was taught that to win the sale, I needed to show enthusiasm and confidence, and that I needed to be persistent and show that I believed in the reason the prospect should buy more than they believed that they shouldn't buy.

Now, please do not misunderstand me here. I can just hear some of you complaining that you don't want to be like a telemarketer, or an obnoxious salesperson, or unprofessional or pushy. Good, because I don't want you to be, either. What I'm talking about is something completely different. Let me explain.

To start with, you must be working with a qualified prospect who has a legitimate interest in your product or service, has a need, is a decision maker, has a budget, and so on. This is the first step. If you don't have all of these things and you begin asking for the sale three to five times or more, then guess what? You're going to become a pushy salesperson.

If you do have these qualifiers in place, then you can feel confident that you're dealing with someone who can and will benefit from your product or service. If that is true, then it is up to you to present value, overcome legitimate stalls and objections, and repeatedly ask for the sale.

You have to remember that many times a prospect is on the fence, and the only way to push him or her off it (and on to your side), is to be persistent and satisfy any doubt or hesitation he or she has with your belief, confidence, and enthusiasm. Here is how you do it.

First, you have to have a set of solid and proven rebuttals for all of the common stalls or objections you are going to get. You must know these responses inside and out so you are not put off when you get them. Remember, if you have to think about how to respond, it is already too late. So many sales reps act like a deer caught in headlights when they get an objection, and because of this, many give up as soon as they do.

You can (and must) avoid that defeated feeling by being prepared with a rebuttal that not only addresses the concern, but that then leads you back into building value and matching up the benefits of your product or service with each prospect's unique buying motives (you know, the ones you uncovered during the qualifying stage). In other words, you need a way back into your pitch. You can use something as simple as:

> "I totally understand how you feel. It does seem that way at first, but actually the way it works is … "

Then continue to build value or discuss a benefit and give them a further reason to buy!

Once you have answered the objection, you must confirm your answer with: "Do you see how that works?" (In other words, use a tie-down.)

If you get a yes, then you ask for the order again: "Then here is what I recommend we do...."

There you have it—you've just asked for the sale again. When you then get another objection or stall, you answer it, confirm your answer, and ask for the sale again! This is the long-lost art of closing the sale. You must be prepared to keep pitching, keep building value, and keep asking for the sale three, five, or even more times.

Now again, for any of you rolling your eyes, you obviously need to be in tune with each prospect, and if someone is getting upset or really isn't going to buy or commit right then, then you back off. I am not suggesting you be pushy or unprofessional in any way, but you have to show belief in your product or service, and you have to be persistent.

Now sometimes a prospect will just go blank and be uninterested for some reason. Perhaps they have already committed to some other company or the budget has gone away, or something else happened. In this case, I recommend you use one of my favorite ways to reopen a dialogue, or at least learn something that will help you keep this from happening in the future with another prospect. I often like to say:

"You know, _____, I love to learn: Do you mind telling me why?"

Then listen very carefully and then connect with what they say, playing off it to reopen the sale.

If you are committed to doing what the other sales reps are not going to do, then I recommend you get your favorite 10 or 15 closes together to handle the five to eight common objections you always get (see Top Characteristic Number 2). Take some time to script them out to match your personality and style so they feel natural to you. Then commit to memorizing them: it helps to record them into your smartphone so you can play this recording of these scripts, in your own voice and with the inflection you want to deliver, over and over again until you have internalized them. Then begin practicing and delivering them automatically each time the selling situation or objection comes up. Once you have these specific rebuttals memorized, then you need to add on some closing statements that automatically direct you to asking for the sale again. Later on, in Chapter Nine "Winning Closing Techniques," you will find some of these specific closing statements.

By combining your rebuttals with closing statements you feel comfortable with, you will then be able to persevere and ask for the sale over and over again. When you begin doing that, something amazing will start to happen: you'll begin closing more sales. You will begin closing prospects who you would have given up on before. Your confidence will go up as you do. Your weekly checks will go up (and you'll love that!). Before you know it, you will have created a whole new skill set and elevated your selling career. You will suddenly be in the Top 20 Percent of your company, and as you revise your pitch even more and get better and better, you'll move into the Top 10 Percent, and then the Top 5 or even Top 1 Percent.

TOP CHARACTERISTIC #8: TREAT GATEKEEPERS WITH COURTESY AND RESPECT

If you have to make cold or warm calls to prospects, then you probably have to deal with your share of gatekeepers. These can be receptionists, office managers, assistants, and so on. No matter what role they have, whoever stands between you and your prospect is someone you have to deal with first.

Most salespeople struggle to effectively deal with and get past these so-called gatekeepers. The majority of the time, the problems they have they bring on themselves. This is because most sales reps treat these people as obstacles to get past by using tricks or by acting authoritatively or by being downright rude, and you can imagine how that goes.

Also, many salespeople simply don't understand some basic rules in regard to how to speak to gatekeepers, so they create their own problems by giving incomplete information, which just triggers the gatekeepers to do their job and keep them away from the decision maker.

Here is a common mistake:

Rep: "Oh hi, is Mr. Jones in?"

Gatekeeper: "May I tell him who is calling?"

Rep: "This is Bob."

Gatekeeper: "Bob who?"

Rep: "Bob Smith."

Gatekeeper: "With what company?"

Rep: "The XYZ company."

Gatekeeper: "Will he know what this call is regarding?"

Rep: "Ah, it's about his (whatever the rep is selling)."

Gatekeeper: "Has he spoken to you before?"

Rep: "Ah, no...."

Once a sales rep gets into that kind of dialogue with a gatekeeper, they rarely win. Over and over again, they will be turned away.

The way to fix all this is easy: always give your first and last name and the company you're calling from right away. Then—and this is crucial—always end with an *instructional statement* like: "Is Bob available, please."

By the way, that is crucial, too: always be polite and use "please"— two or three times even. Here's an effective opening:

Rep: "Hi could I speak with Bob, please?

Gatekeeper: "May I tell him who is calling?"

Rep: "Yes, please. Please tell him that [your first and last name] with [your company name] is holding, please."

If you do this right and with a smile in your voice, you will avoid 80 percent of the screening that you get now. Guaranteed. I know this is effective, because I still use it today and *it works*.

Also, if you don't know a contact's name, use the "I need a little bit of help, please," technique. Always wait for the other person to respond before you ask for it:

Rep: "Hi, I need a little bit of help, please."

(Now pause long enough for the gatekeeper to respond.)

Gatekeeper: "How can I help?"

Rep: "I need to speak with the person who handles your _____. Who would that be, please?"

This is very effective if, again, you say it with a smile in your voice.

Speaking of a smile, always put a *big* smile on your face right before your prospect (or gatekeeper) picks up the phone. It does wonders for how you project your attitude and opening line. In fact, putting a mirror on your desk is very helpful as well. Make sure to look at yourself when the other person answers the phone, and soon you will find yourself speaking with more emotion, energy, and enthusiasm. Before you dismiss this technique, try it for yourself.

By the way, don't be afraid of building a little bit of rapport with the gatekeeper as well.

Ask them if they are happy it's Friday, or how their Monday is going, or if they are glad it's hump day. Ask about the weather. Anything to be personable and to show them that you value them as people rather than as just an obstacle to get around.

The bottom line is that top producers know how to interact with gatekeepers and know how to gain their trust and get them on their side. By using these techniques, you can now begin doing that as well.

Characteristics 9 and 10 both focus on the one trait that is perhaps the most important of all. You find this characteristic in *all* top performers, not just in top sales producers. You see it in top athletes, actors, musicians, dancers, top businesspeople, and so on.

All top producers have this quality in abundant amounts, and parts 9 and 10 will focus on how to develop, grow, protect, and maintain it within a sales context. Here's what it is:

"All top producers develop and maintain a positive, can-and-will-do *attitude*."

TOP CHARACTERISTIC #9: RESIGN FROM THE COMPANY CLUB

What I mean by this is that you have to stay away from the group of salespeople (or even managers) in your office who do nothing but grumble about how bad or unfair things are in your company or about how bad the economy or industry is. You know who and what I am talking about. You usually find them congregating in the break room or hallway or warehouse, or they are outside smoking cigarettes or waiting for the food truck. Many companies have them, and they are poison for your career and your life.

This company club can be made up of average salespeople or a mix of under-producers and unhappy managers who feel they deserve more, or even above-average salespeople who think they should be treated better. They grumble and talk negatively about any and everything: the leads are bad, or marketing is doing a crappy job, or the good leads are being given to the top producers only. They grumble about the product, or the pricing of the product, or the warranty, or durability. They grumble about the office environment, the phone system, the computers, or their desks, or the noise level. They grumble about the commission structure, the salary or benefits, or the bonuses they did or didn't get.

They are generally lazy, or bored, or uninterested, and they set a low standard and drag everyone who will let them down to their level. Instead of focusing on solutions or on making things work, they look for reasons why a new sales campaign or lead source won't work. They are a cancer to all companies, and they are especially deadly to you and your sales attitude.

The answer? Resign from their club.

I remember the club at the company I used to work at. When I was a bottom 80 percent producer, I used to love the club. Every morning the club would meet in the kitchen to eat the free donuts or bagels the company provided. Were we grateful and thankful for the free food and good coffee? No. If they gave us bagels, where was the salmon? If they brought donuts, where were the bagels?

Once we poured our coffee and started in on the free food, we would start in on the leads, or the industry, or the company, or on how the top producers always got preferential treatment. We grumbled our way through the food, grumbled our way back to our desks, and grumbled our way into lunch.

If we missed a sale, we would reconvene in the break room to talk about how we could never sell this stuff with all the things that were wrong with it. How in the world did they expect us to be competitive if they were going to put out such trash? And the leads! On and on we would go until it was finally time to go home. Then we'd grumble to our wives or husbands. As long as I remained a member of that club, my attitude and results were going to suffer.

Everything changed, though, when I made a commitment to become a top producer. Once I had, the first thing I did was resign from the company club. Instead of commiserating with the club, I arrived at the office an hour early and started cold calling or closing leads I had set up the night before. When the club finally wandered in, I often already had a deal on the board and was going for another one. I declined invitations to go to lunch with them, and instead I ate at my desk and rewrote my closes while I listened to my calls and tried to find ways to improve.

When the club members came over to my desk during work hours, I didn't stop calling to talk with them. I went right on calling and working instead. They soon got the hint. When they tried to engage me in the break room, I was pleasant but told them I had to meet my call quota and wanted to get back to work. After a while, they left me alone.

What was interesting is that I noticed that the other top producers acted the same way I now did. They were also the ones who came in early and left late. They were the ones who were more focused on working than chatting, and if they did want to talk, it was usually to strategize a better way of closing a deal. I almost never heard them grumble or talk badly about the company, the industry, or the market.

The top producers (of which group I became a part) were more interested in finding ways to succeed and exceed quota. They didn't mind working harder, or getting help or leveraging management's or each other's experience. When we spoke with one another, it was usually to challenge each other to do better. We competed in a positive way to up each other's game. We shared resources and closing techniques.

What I found is that we had our own club, but it was lightly attended because we had work to do. On those occasions when we did get together, it was to talk about better things like what neighborhood we were moving into, or whether we liked Mercedes or BMW better, or how we were setting up our retirement accounts. These were not the kinds of subjects that were ever discussed in the company club.

What I find even now as a consultant is that many of the companies I work with have a company club. When I'm on site, I can see their members gathering and chitchatting. I also see the top producers at their desks, working away. I've found that top producers are usually loners who are always working, always looking for ways to improve. At the end of my training, the company club members thank me politely (or not at all) and then head off to the break room to talk about what a waste of time the training was.

The top producers, however, are in the training room picking my brain for a new technique, or to discuss one of the scripts or closes I have developed for them. They are thirsty for information, and you can see the commitment on their faces. They are top producers who are always looking for a way to up their game. In fact, when I get back to my office, the Top 1 Percent have often reached out to me to inquire about my one-on-one coaching program. They are willing to pay for it out of their own pockets because they know the investment will pay them many, many times over.

So the question for you is: Are you a part of the company club in your office? If so, then resign today and start finding ways to build your attitude rather than spending your time ripping it down. And you can begin building your attitude up by following Top Characteristic Number 10.

TOP CHARACTERISTIC #10: INVEST DAILY IN YOUR ATTITUDE

Now that you have resigned from the company club, you can use that time and energy to do the one thing that will have the most impact on your performance and your life: invest in ways to build up your attitude on a daily basis. Before we get in to some ways to do that, let me emphasize the importance of investing time and energy *every day* to improving, strengthening, and elevating your attitude. The "every day" part is the key. Think about it: How many times a day do you eat? If you are like most people, then you probably eat three times a day and have some snacks in between. Now let me ask you: If you skipped breakfast, how would you be feeling by, say, 11 A.M.? Cranky? Hungry? Unable to concentrate much? How about if you also skipped lunch that day? How would you be feeling around, say, 3:30 P.M.? Would you be ready for that big presentation? Or that meeting with your sales manager or boss?

Okay, now let's say you got home by 6 P.M. and you hadn't eaten anything all day. How would you be around your wife and kids? (Or roommate or girl/boyfriend or dog?) Would *you* want to be around you? Now imagine going two days without food. Try three. I think we could all agree you'd be pretty much worthless by then (if not way before!).

The reason I bring this up is that your mind, your attitude, needs feeding just like your body does. If you don't make a concerted effort to feed it regularly, then it, too, will get sluggish and worthless pretty soon. If you don't spend active time feeding your mind, feeding your attitude positive material, then you will be more susceptible to negativity, more susceptible to members of the club, and each time you have a bad outcome—client doesn't reload, new prospect doesn't buy, you don't make your lead numbers—you will get more and more discouraged.

And if you let that happen, then you will begin searching for reasons why you won't succeed.

And if you let that continue, you will either find them or you will make them up.

Top producers make it a priority to consciously feed their minds positive stories and positive examples, and they cultivate a can-do, positive attitude. They spend time taking in other positive thinkers' ideas and strategies, and they purposefully employ those strategies in their lives. They listen to audio books, or they read (or reread) books on how to get better and do better. Many top performers also spend time with affirmations and visualizations linked to purposeful and motivating goal setting. All this pays off. Those producers who are in the habit of developing a vision, and who dedicate themselves to achieving it—no matter what—those are the top producers, the top athletes, and other top performers who always outperform their competition.

But it all starts by making a commitment to developing, feeding and cultivating a positive, can-do attitude. The key, again, is to do this daily (several times a day, actually). So how do you get into the habit of doing this? A good start is to find the medium that works best for you. If you are a reader, then get some books that resonate with you and commit to reading a certain amount of pages each day. If you prefer audio books, then get those books on MP3 and listen to them on the way to and from work, or when you get home, or at the gym, or when you're walking the dog.

One resource I still work with today are subliminal recordings. Subliminal recordings are great because they speak right to your sub-conscious mind, which runs just about everything in your life. I listen to recordings either during meditation or during relaxation sessions. I also use them to help me go to sleep on a regular basis. A great resource for these can be found here: http://www.instant-hypnosis.com/?afl=69646.

Just browse the sections and download a few to get started. I'll tell you now, it's much better to lie in bed listening to one of the powerful recordings than to lie in bed worrying about your income!

Another good thing to do is to pick up a few books or audio programs on setting goals. Just listing what it is you're going to accomplish this year (or in the next six months) can be highly motivating by itself. As soon as you define your vision, you will find that you begin to automatically feel more positive and motivated. When setting goals, just remember: "*Whatever you want to have or achieve is possible. Other people around the world have and have achieved the very thing that lives in your heart. If they can have it and do it, so can you!*"

But you will need to work for it first. You will need to rearrange your consciousness so that it can embrace the new expectation of what you come to believe is possible. And this is where affirmations are crucial.

Affirmations are simply statements or images that you feed yourself, thoughts and emotions that you tend to dwell on throughout the day and night. Everybody already uses affirmations—you're using them right now. The problem is that most people are using the wrong affirmations and getting the things they don't want as a result. The reason for this is that most people's random self-talk is incredibly negative. That is where affirmations come in. Affirmations are nothing more than carefully constructed words, phrases, and stories that you design in advance that support the goals you've identified are important to you.

There are many books on this subject, and you can easily do a search to find the one(s) that speak to you. Affirmations are key to help you feel positive about yourself and your career and maintain the positive attitude that will enable you to persevere and succeed.

With all of the resources mentioned here: books, CDs/MP3s, subliminal recordings, goal setting, affirmations, and so forth, you will be able to put together a varied and full course of "food for your attitude" that you will be able to munch on throughout your day. If you are not doing this now, or have stopped doing it, then start today. It is amazing how just a little bit of positive energy can turn around a day, a week, a month, or a whole life. Remember, all top producers have a positive, can-do attitude. If you don't believe me, then get around some of them—their attitude is contagious. Yours needs to be, too.

In ending this section on the Top Ten Characteristics of Top Sales Producers, I hope you have seen some ideas that resonate and that you feel will work for you. Just adopting a few of these habits will have an immediate and dramatic effect on your career in sales, and on your life in general. I hope you have already adopted some of the characteristics, and you already know how valuable they are. Make a commitment today to put even more of them to work for yourself. I guarantee that the more you use, the better you will feel and perform.

PART II

PROSPECTING TECHNIQUES AND SCRIPTS

CHAPTER 2

Better, Smarter Prospecting Techniques

New Cold Calling Techniques That Work

L earning how to effectively pick up the phone and make an effective cold (or prospecting) call is *the* most important sales skill you can learn. Every other part of the sale follows this essential skill. If you are not closing sales the way you want to be, then it can invariably be traced back to a poor job of qualifying a lead during the prospecting phase of the sale. If you put in the time to learn and perfect the art of cold calling, your results can quickly change. Once you get good at prospecting, you grow in confidence, your sales improve dramatically, and you truly put your career and future in your own hands. No other skill is more important than learning how to effectively call a prospect, build rapport, and then know how to deal with and bypass their initial resistance. No skill is more important than knowing how to truly qualify a sales prospect.

I say this is the most important skill, yet I know some of you will want to argue that closing is the most important skill. This is not true. "You can't close an unqualified lead" is the most important tenet in sales. Unfortunately, that's what entire sales teams are attempting to do every day: close leads that are not qualified and therefore will never close. Managers spend much of their day monitoring and measuring what goes into the sales funnel, and new software is developed (and purchased) to measure the top of the funnel, the middle, and the bottom. Metrics are carefully collected and analyzed in an attempt to diagnose and fix the "sales problem" as it relates to the sales funnel, yet no one is looking at or attempting to fix the most important part: what goes *into* the funnel to begin with!

There is an old adage that I'm sure you have heard before: "Garbage in, garbage out." This is the most accurate way to describe most companies'—and sales reps'—pipelines. The average rate of closed sales from supposedly qualified leads—leads that a sales rep has prospected for, put into his or her pipeline, and given presentations to—is two out of 10. That means that *just two leads* turn into deals, while the other eight are abandoned. Think about the time, energy, and resources that go into those eight failed sales! This is why companies need to look at the real problem instead of investing in ways to measure, calculate, and endlessly discuss these abominable results.

The real problem is that companies, sales managers, and trainers (if the company is lucky enough to have a trainer) often don't know how to properly teach the fundamental sales skills to begin with. This is especially true with cold calling and qualifying. The essential skills that you'll find in this book seem to be a lost art. I am hired by companies all the time—very successful ones, too—and when I do my discovery, drill down to their sales process, and look at the actual techniques and scripts they give their sales reps to use while cold calling and qualifying, they are abysmal. Very few companies give their sales teams actual scripted approaches, strategies, and tools to handle the selling situations they run into day after day. Most sales teams are ill prepared to handle the resistance they constantly get, and fewer still have any real criteria as to what constitutes a "qualified lead" to begin with. Given this dearth of techniques, skills, and guidance, it's no wonder that sales teams fail, morale is low, and turnover is so high. The only thing it does explain is why the conversion rate is so low—again, about 20 percent across industries.

So what is the solution? The solution is to recognize what I said at the beginning of this book: the best thing about sales is that 80 percent of the selling situations, resistance, stalls, and objections a sales rep and team get are the same day in and day out. In other words, sales are repeatable processes with recurring objections and stalls. The solution for improvement of sales results is the same for an individual sales rep as with the entire sales team: you need to learn, adapt, internalize, and use proven and effective sales skills, techniques, and scripts to effectively and confidently deal with these recurring sales situations. In other words, selling is a predictable process, and by carefully preparing for it, you and your team can successfully predict (and improve) your results.

What I do for all my clients is first identify the best-practice sales process for their product or service, then create a comprehensive script playbook that follows this best-practice approach. Many of those exact scripts and techniques are what you're going to find in this book. Once you create this best-practice approach to handling your specific sale, that's when you go from ad-libbing (the "spray and pray" approach to pitching), to becoming a prepared professional who knows exactly how to create a qualified prospect and then lead that prospect through to a closed sale. Once you learn to do that, you greatly increase your lead-to-close ratio, and your team begins closing closer to five out of 10 leads. Your top reps will get closer to five out of eight sales per lead ratio. That's when you'll know you have created not only a successful sales process, but one that you can scale as well.

It all starts here, at the beginning. It all starts with your very first call: the prospecting call. Learning how to handle the key, repeatable situations here will form the groundwork for everything else you will do. Learning how to confidently handle blow-offs that frustrate the other 80 percent of sales reps who are winging it, and learning how to truly develop rapport by actively engaging prospects, and then learning how to professionally qualify them so you know exactly what their buying motives are, what their true timeline is, and why they will or will not choose you—these are the real parts that should be measured in a sales pipeline. Once you do, the other numbers so many managers focus on now—the top, middle, and end of the funnel—will sort themselves out. Because finally, true closing ratios will change for the better.

What you will find in the paragraphs that follow are fresh approaches to cold calling and qualifying techniques that are being used effectively today by some of the best sales teams in the world. Many of these are advanced techniques, and in this book I have not gone over the same ground I covered in my first book of scripts, *The Ultimate Book of Phone Scripts*. That book, too, is packed with essential and proven techniques that will help you deal with the gatekeeper and overcome initial resistance and objections. I highly recommend you invest time and energy incorporating those proven scripts as well. Together, these two books of phone scripts and techniques will give you and your team every script, strategy, and skill you will need to successfully navigate any sales process.

Now, don't worry—you will find a plethora of proven and effective scripts in this book to help you prospect, qualify, and effectively deal with the objections you get now while calling. These scripts are proven effective, and they are the same ones I use in both my business and my training. Your goal as a sales rep or sales leader is to read these scripts and then take the time to adapt them to your product or service and to your personality. It is crucial that you customize these scripts by tweaking them so they feel natural to you. Once you do, it's time to record them into a recording device (most smart phones have a recording feature) and listen to them 30 to 40 times. That way, you will memorize and internalize them. After you use them 50 times or more, they will become a habit for you and the way you just automatically respond to the selling situations and objections you get over and over.

Once you do that, sales will become easy for you. Once you don't have to think about how to respond to a prospect, that's when success becomes automatic for you. Suddenly you will find that you can actually listen to your prospects and hear not only what they are saying, but also what they really mean. That is when you've entered the Top 20 Percent of the sales producers in the world. From there, you only get better and better, faster and faster. Once you put in the time to learn the scripts and techniques in this book, your sales career, your life, and your company will never be the same. It's exciting, and I'm excited for you. So, if you are ready, keep an open mind as you read the following scripts and techniques, and constantly ask yourself: How does this technique or script apply to what *I* am selling? How can I customize it so it is effective for me?

If you keep yourself focused on the similarities rather than the differences (a good philosophy, by the way, for all of life), you will keep yourself focused on improving and getting better. It all starts with the following solid scripts and techniques you will read here.

A FRESH PROSPECTING APPROACH FOR YOU

Like you, I get calls every week from inside sales reps trying to sell me their products and services. I used to just hang up on them, noting that I wasn't missing much, as most inside sales reps are just not that good at engaging, listening, building rapport, and so on. Lately, however, I have been listening more and realizing that I can learn just as much from a bad call as I can from a good one. I recently received a qualifying call from an appointment setter, and it turned out to be a fresh approach I'd not heard before. I picked up a couple of good ideas, and if this approach can be adapted to your sale, I would highly recommend you try it.

Here's what happened: the call I received was from a company selling some sort of oil and gas drilling private placement investment. For those of you unfamiliar with these, this is the kind of investment that a private company can sell directly to an individual investor. In other words, the company usually (and I use "usually" very loosely—check with your individual state governing body) doesn't have to register with the Securities and Exchange Commission, and so can "usually" avoid a ton of administrative and regulatory red tape.

The big "but" here is that this type of investment vehicle can generally only be offered to, and sold to, what is known as an "accredited" investor, meaning someone who has at least a $1 million net worth and income in excess of $200,000. (Again, if you deal in these kinds of investments, check with your state regulatory agency for the specific guidelines for your state and the states you are calling.)

The company that contacted me used a "qualifier" whose job it is to call and qualify people as an accredited investor before any sales rep speaks with them. Using a qualifier to simply identify potential prospects was a good idea, as it no doubt saved the sales reps a lot of time and effort. This is good, and one I'd not heard before. Here is how the call went:

> Caller: "Hi, my name is Sonya, and I'm calling with the ABC Oil and Gas Company here in Dallas, Texas. Am I speaking with Mike Brooks?"
>
> Me: "Ah, yes. . . ."

Caller: "Mike, this is not a sales call at all. I only have two quick questions for you, and then I'll go, okay?"

Me: "Sure, go ahead."

Caller: "We have in our records that you are an accredited investor with a net worth of at least one million dollars, right?"

Me: "Sure."

Caller: "And is your income still at least $200,000 or over?"

Me: "Sure."

Caller: "Okay, great. One of our representatives will be in touch with you in the next few days. Thanks for your time, and have a good day."

And that was it. She was gone almost as quickly as she appeared. In the span of just a couple of minutes, she had qualified me enough to pass me on (as a lead) to one of the closers. Very interesting. Let's break down why this was so effective:

1. She made sure she was speaking to the decision maker before she continued: "Am I speaking to Mike Brooks?"

2. She sensed my hesitancy and immediately had a reply for it: "Mike, this is not a sales call at all. . . ."

3. Next, she earned the right to ask just two questions because she then said she would be off the phone: "I have only two quick questions for you, and then I'll go, okay?"

4. Then she qualified me for the two most important criteria for her sale—net worth and income.

5. The ending was interesting. She told me that someone else would be following up in a few days, and before I could object, she hung up.

I am not saying I love this call or hate it. I am just impressed by how efficient it was in qualifying, and how quickly she could generate a lead and then pass it on. Obviously, these two qualifiers are crucial to know before one of their sales reps gets involved, and this turned out to be an effective way to do it.

Now, how could you use this technique in your sale? First, if you work with appointment setters, lead gen reps, or qualifiers, then pick out the two most important qualifications and use the preceding script to create your pitch for your initial callers. Here are three examples.

If you are selling lead or marketing services, it could be:

1. "Do you handle the lead generation for marketing?"

2. "If you plan to compare services or companies in the next quarter, would you be open to reviewing material from another company?"

If you are selling online advertising, it could be:

1. "How much do you get involved in the online advertising decisions?"

2. "Are you open to at least knowing about options to improve your current results while perhaps also saving money?"

If you are selling real estate, it could be:

1. "Are you the homeowner?"

2. "Do you have any plans to consider selling your home in the next 12 months?"

You get the idea. Almost any product or service has a couple of key questions that a qualifier can ask to prequalify a lead. The best part of this script is that it takes under a minute! You are on and then off with a prospect very quickly, and, as I found, the prospect is left somewhat expecting the next call, whether they want it or not. For the next two weeks, every time the phone rang, I half expected it to be the oil and gas rep! So, what are the two most important qualifiers for your sale, and how can you get your lead gen people to ask them quickly and efficiently?

A Better Approach Than "How Are You Today?"

Nothing signals a sales call more than that worn-out opening, "How are you today?" As soon as you ask that of someone you've not spoken to before, their immediate thought is, "Oh, here comes a sales pitch from someone I don't want to talk to!"

If you don't believe me, think about your own reaction when someone you don't know calls you at home or the office and asks you that? I cringe just thinking about it, and so do your prospects. Wouldn't you like to know a better opening? Wouldn't you like to find something that doesn't sound sales-y, yet still breaks the ice and gets your prospect to respond positively?

Well, I have it for you.

I learned this opening working with a new client recently, and while at first I was suspicious of whether it would work or not, after listening to recordings, I found that it worked really well. So well, in fact, that I now teach it to other clients, and it works great for them as well.

As you'll see, it is assumptive in nature (always a good thing); it gets your prospect to agree with you, and it puts you in control, allowing you to continue your opening. Use it word for word for a week, and I think you will agree:

"Hi _____, this is _____ with [your company]. I trust you are doing well today?"

If you would like to vary it a little, you can also say:

"Hi _____, this is _____ with [your company]. I take it you're doing well today?"

or

"Hi _____, this is _____ with [your company]. I hope your day is going well so far?"

As you can see, this opening invariably leads to a yes, and even a response of, "Yes, and I hope yours is, too."

The big difference here is that you are finally going to stop sounding like every other sales rep out there, and you are going to stop telegraphing that your call is another sales call.

As with all these scripts, don't take my word for it—try it yourself and see how it works for you. I am sure, with a little practice, you will love how effective it is.

DON'T SAY THAT, SAY THIS!

I always say that sales is set of repeatable skills that anyone can learn. If you commit to learning and practicing the right skills, then things will be easier for you and you will have more success, but if you don't learn and use the right skills, then you will tend to wing it and make things up as you go along. This strategy is proven to lead to more frustration and fewer sales. It's sad but true: most sales reps use ineffective skills and techniques that make it harder for them to succeed. Until you change what you do, you will just keep getting those poor results.

Following are five examples of poor techniques. I call them "Don't say that," followed by what to say instead. Look at these and ask yourself how many of these you are using and then make a commitment to begin using the more effective statements instead. Give these a test for a while and see for yourself how much easier selling over the phone becomes.

While prospecting, don't say:

"I wonder if I caught you at a good time?"

Or

"Is this a good time for you?"

While it sounds polite to ask permission before you begin a conversation, giving your prospect a chance to avoid speaking to a salesperson (you) is almost always a bad idea. If I am ever given that option, I always say it's a bad time just to get you off the phone. There is a better way to acknowledge that you are barging into someone's day unannounced.

Say this instead:

"I know you're busy, so let me briefly ask you just one thing: we provide (your product) to other companies or clients, and it may help you, too. I have a quick question: How do you currently...."

Or

"When was the last time you compared...."

Or

"Are you the right person to speak with regarding this?"

This technique works on several levels: first, you are acknowledging that they are busy and letting them know in advance that you are going to be brief. Second, the opening is short, and you immediately engage your prospect by asking a qualifying question. By getting to a question quickly, you are giving your prospect the opportunity to tell you if he or she is busy or not. And don't worry, if they don't have the time, they will tell you. This is much better than offering them the easy out in the beginning. Third, by asking a qualifying question (and feel free to customize what you want to ask), you are learning something about your prospect. Overall, this is the much more effective opening, and I encourage you to give it a fair trial.

While prospecting, don't say:

"I'm calling to learn a little bit more about your company...."

Quick: What is the one thing you and your prospects don't have enough of? Time. One of the biggest causes of resistance from your prospects is the idea of a sales rep taking some of their precious time to pitch them on something they probably don't want anyway. I groan when a sales rep calls me and starts pitching. When you are at home and a telemarketer calls you, how do *you* feel?

While opening your call by asking, "I'm calling to learn a little bit more about your company," might sound consultative and in your prospect's best interest, it isn't perceived that way. It is instead like saying, "I'm a sales rep who wants to take your valuable time and interrogate you so I can learn whether I can sell you something." Not very appealing, is it? That's why it's much better to say this instead:

"_____, briefly, we help companies do (training, software, and so on), and I just have a quick question to easily find out if this is a fit for you as well.

"How do you currently...."

Or

"When was the last time you...."

Or

"Are you the right person to speak with regarding this?"

Once again, the key is to be brief and to get to a qualifying question quickly. Your prospect will appreciate that you're getting to the point right away, and this immediately separates you from all the other sales reps calling to steal their time.

While prospecting, don't open your call like this:

"The reason for my call is that we provide accounting solutions for companies that process more than 150 employees in a month. Our solution is ideal for companies like yours in that we can save you both time and money handling...."

Believe it or not, most sales reps start a call with a product dump monologue that instantly puts prospects in a bad mood. Nobody cares what you do or how you do it. Instead, what they want to know is if it is a fit for them and how it can help them. That is why you must—absolutely must—get to the point quickly and ask them a question so they can *engage with you.*

Do open your call this way instead:

"The reason I'm calling is to see if you'd be a good candidate for what we do.... In a nutshell, we have a super-easy solution that saves companies as much as 15 percent monthly in the way they process their employee checks. Let me ask you just two quick questions:

One: Who are you using now to process employee payments?

Two: If we could also save you 15 percent off your monthly expenses, how open would you be to seeing if this would be a fit for you?"

This opening is much better for several reasons. First, it is short (always a good thing on a prospecting call). Next, it lets them know you are simply calling to see if they would be a fit (which is what they want to know as well before they're willing to invest more time to speak with you). It also tells them your solution is "super easy" (and who doesn't like that?). Then it gives them a benefit (the 15 percent). Lastly, you are immediately giving them an opportunity to interact by asking a question and letting them talk.

While prospecting, don't say:

"Are you the person who would be making a decision on something like this?"

The biggest problem with this approach is that it is closed-ended. It requires a yes or no answer, and that allows the prospect to hide behind a smokescreen answer. It is much easier for them to say yes and avoid getting into the real decision tree that you will unfortunately find out later. (Like when you ask for the sale and they tell you they should run this by their boss, manager, spouse, and so on.)

Say this instead:

"Besides yourself, who else weighs in on a decision like this?"

Ah, the power of open-ended, assumptive questions. This question immediately cuts through any smokescreen your prospect would otherwise use, and it automatically gets them to reveal who else is involved. Most people will consult with someone (or multiple people) when making a decision. Don't you? Isn't it better to find out in advance who those people are?

While closing, don't respond to the objection:

"I'll run this by my regional manager (or boss or partner, and so forth) and see what he or she says."

With:

"When should I get back to you?"

So much time and energy can be saved if you prepare yourself for this common stall in advance by learning how to answer it correctly.

The last thing you want to do is hand control of the close over to your prospect by asking when you should get back to them.

While closing, do respond to this objection this way:

"Terrific, and if he gives you the okay to move on this, what other questions do you have for me?"

Or

"Okay, and let me ask you: Based on what you've seen so far, is this something that you'd be inclined to move forward with if the decision were up to you?"

(If yes)

"And how much influence do you have with your regional manager in deciding on something like this?"

I can't emphasize enough that one of the biggest keys to success in sales is to realize that 80 percent of the objections you get are the same ones you got yesterday and that you will get again tomorrow. In other words, most of the selling situations, objections, and stalls you get remain the same! Once you acknowledge this, you can leverage this by taking the time to prepare in advance with the right responses to the stalls and objections you get all the time. The preceding response allows you to isolate the stall at the end of your close and get right to the real objection. In other words, if the prospect isn't sold, then speaking to someone else is just a smokescreen that won't go away when you call them back. Finding out now gives you the ability to deal with the real objection, and it is best to do so while you have them on the phone and you are in the closing arena.

As you can see by these techniques, sales is a series of definable and repeatable skills that anyone can learn. The key, however, is to make a commitment to learning and then consistently applying the right skills until they become your automatic habit. Remember, practice doesn't make perfect; *it only makes permanent*. If you use poor skills over and over, you are not going to improve. Conversely, making small adjustments in the techniques you use can have a *big* impact on your results.

But do not take my word for it. As always, try these scripts for yourself and see how much better a reaction you get, and how much more easily your cold calling and closing presentations go.

How to Develop an Effective Elevator Pitch

Many inside sales reps (outside reps, too!) struggle when trying to describe their company, products, and services in a succinct and compelling way that engages a prospect and makes them want to hear more. Instead, a typical opening delivered to an unsuspecting prospect usually sounds more like a monologue meant to repel interest and generate the impulse to get off the phone as soon as possible. I am sure you have been accosted in this way with something like:

> "Oh hi, this is _____ with _____ and my company, XYZ, is a leader in national and international shipping and freight services with offices in the top metropolitan cities across the world. We offer one of the lowest overall freight charges on transportation, and also on packaging and supplies. We are going to have a representative in your city next week, and we'd love to stop by to share some information with you and learn more about your business to see how we can help save you money and time as well. Would you be available next Wednesday at 2 P.M., or would Thursday at 4 P.M. be better?"

And companies and sales reps wonder why they are not successful. Rather than break down what is wrong with this opening (how about everything?), what I am going to do instead is give you two rules for developing an effective elevator pitch and then some examples that you can plug your product or service into.

Here are the two rules:

1. Make it brief—one sentence is best, two short ones if necessary.

2. Focus it on the direct benefits to your specific type of customer.

Remember, this is an "elevator pitch" designed to inform and grab interest in a prospect during the time you are in an elevator together. Try working with the following examples.

Elevator pitch example 1:

"_____, we work with small business owners helping them save on average 20 percent of their shipping costs while also increasing their efficiency and tracking. To see how we can help you, I'd like to schedule a brief 10-minute meeting next week...."

Elevator pitch example 2:

"_____, we help inside sales teams achieve as much as 33 percent more monthly revenue by providing them with a best-practice approach that helps them cold-call more effectively and close more qualified prospects. This means an immediate bump in production and profits, often within the first 30 days."

Elevator pitch example 3:

"_____ the ABC Company gives homeowners complete peace of mind by eliminating routine maintenance costs and insuring against unexpected expenses. I've got just two questions to see which of our plans might work for you...."

Elevator pitch example 4:

"_____, our motto is: "A guaranteed comfortable night's sleep, or your money back." Now, have you ever tried our luxury brand of mattress before?"

Elevator pitch example 5:

"_____, at (training, software, and so on) advertising, our small business clients get the most comprehensive online exposure, the certified highest traffic, and the most qualified leads in the industry—all at the guaranteed lowest rates. Where are you currently advertising online now?"

As you can see by these elevator pitches, not only are they short and focused on the benefits to a specific customer ("small business owner" or "homeowner"), they often end with a qualifying question like "Have you ever tried....?" or "Where are you currently advertising online now?"

By ending with a qualifying question, you are not only engaging your prospect, but you are also learning about their buying motives and uncovering their level of interest. Take some time now to develop your own concise and compelling elevator pitch, and then replace your monologue with a more effective opening. Your customers (and your bank account) will thank you for it.

FOUR WAYS TO GET PAST THE GATEKEEPER

Getting screened out by the receptionist or gatekeeper is still one of the biggest causes of phone aversion. Questions like, "Will he know who's calling?" or "Will he know what this call is about," or "Has she spoken to you before?" are enough to keep any inside sales rep up at night, and the sad thing is it doesn't have to be this way! If you follow the basic philosophy provided here and then adapt and use any of the scripts provided, you can instantly increase your transfer rate to the decision maker.

The basic philosophy on getting gatekeepers to put you through is this: stop trying to hide. Don't try to trick or fool the gatekeeper into thinking that you already know or have spoken to the prospect before. Also, stop inviting the gatekeeper to interrogate you by giving them incomplete information like just your first name, or by not giving them your company name in the beginning. And most of all, *stop pitching the gatekeeper*. It also helps to remember what the gatekeeper's role is.

A gatekeeper's role is to find out the name and company name of the person calling so they can let the decision maker (DM) know who is on the line. In most cases, that's it. In reality (and most of the time), they don't need to know if you have a relationship with the DM or not, or what you are selling, and so on. If you volunteer this information in the beginning (rather than making them drag it out of you) and you do it in a polite and assumptive way, you will get put through to the decision maker without any additional screening. Use the following proven techniques to fly by the receptionist or gatekeeper and be connected directly with the decision maker most of the time.

Technique 1: Please, please, please. I have written about this technique before, but it remains the most effective and easiest one to use to increase your chances of being put through up to 65 to 75 percent of the time. (I still use this every single day, and it *works!*) Here is how it goes:

> Receptionist: "Thanks for calling the ABC Company. How can I help you?"
>
> You: "Hi, this is _____ with [your company name], may I please speak with _____, please?"

That's it. Simple, easy, and very effective. The key is to say this with a warm smile in your voice, and make sure you use "please" twice along with the instructional statement: "May I please speak with...." The other key is that you give your full name and your full company name as well (even if it doesn't mean anything to them).

Technique 2: If you don't know the name of the contact you need to speak with, then use the "I need a little help, please," technique. It is very effective if you do it the way I describe here.

> Receptionist: "Thanks for calling the ABC Company. How can I help you?"
>
> You: "Hi _____, this is _____ with [your company name]. I need a little bit of help, please." [It is crucial that you *wait* here for the person to ask how they can help you before you ask for the person or department.]
>
> Receptionist: "How can I help you?"
>
> You: "I need to speak with the best person who handles (your product or service). Who would that be, please?"

Over 50 percent of the time, if you have asked this nicely enough and waited for a response, the receptionist will route you to the right department. When you get there, simply use the previous opening again, and you will be consistently connected with the right contact.

The key here is to: be polite and put a smile in your voice; say "please," and make sure to *wait* for the person to respond before you ask for the right person. This will work if you follow the preceding three steps.

Technique 3: If you don't know the name of the contact, an alternative is to ask to be put through to a department instead, and then use the preceding technique. This is a great way to completely bypass the gatekeeper and avoid any chance of screening.

> Receptionist: "Thanks for calling the ABC Company. How can I help you?"

> You: "Hi, could you please connect me with the marketing department, please?"

Again, be assumptive and use that powerful word, "please."

Once you get there, use the "I need a little bit of help, please" technique.

Technique 4: If you get screened further, you absolutely *must* know exactly how to respond. Use any of the following techniques:

> If the receptionist asks: "Is he expecting your call?"

> You answer: "I don't have an appointment this time, but could you please tell him that _____ is holding, please?"

> If the receptionist asks: "Will he know what this call is about?"

> You answer: "Not specifically, but please tell him it's about [his lead tracking], and I'll be happy to hold on, please."

You can also substitute "not specifically" with any of the following: "not yet. . . ." or "not sure," and so on.

A key point here is that you resist the urge to *pitch the receptionist*. So many inside sales reps think that if they only tell the gatekeeper how great their product or service is, then they will want to put you through. This is a *big* mistake! First, remember that the gatekeeper doesn't care what you are selling—they just need your name and company name so they have something to give the decision maker (in most cases). Second, as soon as you launch into a sales pitch, you immediately identify yourself as a sales rep, and this raises a red flag for them. Instead, use "please" and always end with an instructional statement asking to be put through (please!).

> If the receptionist asks: "Have you spoken to him before?"

> You answer: "Not about [his lead tracking], but could you please let him know that _____ with _____ is holding, please?"

Do not mistake how simple these techniques seem—they are powerful, and they work *if* you deliver them warmly and exactly as stated. Remember, a gatekeeper's main goal isn't to screen you out, but rather to pass on accurate information on who is calling, and from what company, and sometimes what the call is regarding. Will you run into some gatekeepers who are harder to get through? Of course. Will these techniques work all the time? Of course not, but if you use them consistently, you'll find that they will work with about 70 percent of the companies you call. I bet that is a higher percentage than your current techniques are producing, isn't it?

WHY ASKING FOR HELP IS A GREAT WAY TO GET INFORMATION

Before you discount the technique of politely asking for help, just remember that everyone loves to be helpful. I am sure you feel better when you hold the door open for someone at the supermarket or if you let someone pull into traffic in front of you. By recognizing this, you will have a greater opportunity to get through to the right department or contact if you enlist the help of the gatekeeper or receptionist first.

Here are some expanded examples of how asking for help at the right time can do more than just get you through to the right person or department. If you play it right, you can also get a treasure trove of useful information you can use to position your product or service later on.

As stated in the preceding section, if you don't know the person or department you need to speak with, there is no better opening than:

"Hi, I need a little bit of help, please.…"

Once again, the crucial thing here is not to ask a question. (It is amazing how many people just can't resist asking one right away! If this describes you, then hit your mute button *right after* you ask for help.) As soon as they say, "What do you need?" or "I can help you," that's when you reply with something like:

"Thanks. I'm looking for the person who handles [your lead generation]. Who would that be, please?"

If they don't know the name, then be prepared with:

"Perhaps you could point me to the right department then?"

Asking for help in this way is also useful when you ask for someone and he or she is no longer there. It is also great for when you do reach someone and he or she turns out to be the wrong contact. When that happens, use:

"Oh, I see. Perhaps you can help me then. Who would be the best person to speak with regarding _____?"

Or

"I see. Can you point me in the right direction then, please?"

Or

"Okay, perhaps you can help me. Who would be the right person for me to speak with about ordering your (training, software, and so on) supplies?"

These techniques are great for finding the right person or department to speak with, but the power of this technique goes far beyond that. Use the following types of "help" questions once you do reach the appropriate prospect:

"I'm glad I got in touch with you. Perhaps you can help me understand how you handle your (training, software, and so on) process. How do you get involved in that?"

Or

"I'm glad I got in touch with you. Perhaps you can help me. How does the ordering of the (training, software, and so on) process go?"

And

"_____, we have a lot of solutions that may be a fit, but I don't want to bombard you. Perhaps you can help give me a brief understanding of who handles what, and then I'll be able to know who would be the best person for this. Let's start with you—what do you take care of there?"

And

"_____, could you help me understand how this flows at your company? Who handles (training, software, and so on)?"

And

"_____, help me understand how the decision process works over there. How do you get involved?"

And

"Perhaps you can help me. I'm sure you've got a lot of people handling different things. Let's start with the part of the process you handle. What part is that?"

Layer with:

"And who handles the other parts?"

As you can see, there are a lot of applications for the "I need a little bit of help, please" technique. Now, a word of caution: don't underestimate how powerful this is. While it seems simple, it is actually a very powerful technique if you use it appropriately.

One more tip: when asking for help, genuinely mean it. Use your voice inflection and timing. Remember to always wait for the other person to offer to help you! If you master this technique, you will find that you won't have to work so hard to find things out. Because they sincerely want to help, people will help you—if you ask correctly.

STOP PITCHING THE GATEKEEPER—AND WHAT TO DO INSTEAD

One of the biggest mistakes many inside sales reps make is pitching the gatekeeper. For some reason, they feel compelled to pour their pitch on the first pair of ears they get, and, unfortunately, this usually gets them into trouble.

To start with, the gatekeeper is just that—someone whose job it is to screen salespeople from getting through to the decision maker. The worst thing you can do is immediately identify yourself as a salesperson by pitching them in the hope that they will be so moved by your pitch that they will want to put you through right away. Doesn't happen. Instead, all you do is trigger their automatic response of, "Just email something, and I'll forward it to my boss." Or worse.

Also, the reason you don't want to pitch the gatekeeper is because they don't care what you are selling and they usually have zero say in whether to buy from you or not. Again, they are gatekeepers—not decision makers. Pitching them will mean nothing, and all it will do is annoy them and waste your time.

So, what to do? Your job, believe it or not, is to get past the gatekeeper with as little interrogation as possible and connect with the decision maker. That is the person you want to give your brief pitch to. So here are a couple of ways to avoid pitching the gatekeeper, and instead, getting to the decision maker.

1. By now, you know all about the "Please, please, please" technique. Some of you are already using it, and isn't it great? For those of you who aren't yet—what's wrong with you? It is amazingly effective! You can avoid 65 percent (or more) of any screening by simply opening your call with:

"Hi, this is [your name] with [your company], could you please connect me with [DM's name], please?"

That's it. To learn more about this technique, visit my blog here: http://mrinsidesales.com/insidesalestrainingblog

2. If you do not know the name of the person you are looking for, simply say:

"Hi, this is [your name] with [your company] and I need a little bit of help, please."

After they ask how they can help you, you say,

"I'm looking for the person who handles (training, software, and so on). Who would that be, please?"

That is it. No pitching and no pleading to be put through. Instead, you are simply asking for their help and then directing them to put you through. If you ask this in a polite way, you will get through most of the time.

Now here comes the tricky part: in some cases, the gatekeeper has a little more authority, like an office manager or executive assistant. In these cases, it is okay to deliver your opening value statement briefly—just so they know what it is about—but then it is highly important to try to get through to the decision maker as soon as possible. Here are a few ways to do that.

The best way is to quickly qualify for decision-maker status. As soon as you ask if he or she makes the decision on what you are selling and are told that someone else makes the decision, that is your cue to ask to be put through to the actual DM. By the way, never say, "decision maker." Rather, use the contact's name. Try:

"Oh, I see. I'll tell you what: if you would put me through to [DM—contact's name] briefly, I'll explain what this is about, and if he (or she) is interested in learning more, I can make an appointment that fits his/her schedule. I will be happy to hold on while you connect me."

Or

"It sounds like the best thing to do before I send something is to have just a few words with [DM], and that way I can save us both a lot of time depending on their level of interest. Could you please let [DM] know that I'm holding, please?"

Or

"Before I bother you with emails and then follow-up calls, why don't you put me in touch with [the boss/DM] briefly, and I will see if there is an interest on his/her side. If so, I will take the appropriate action. If not, we will save us all a lot of time. Could you let [the DM] know I'm holding, please?"

Sometimes the gatekeeper or office manager will want a little more information on what it is you are offering, and in this case, it is okay to give them more details, but just make sure that you qualify for their role in the decision process, and that you ask for the best way to connect with the other decision makers, if possible. Sample questions include: "And besides yourself, who makes the decision on this?"

Layer with:

"Great, may I connect briefly with them to make sure this is something they would like to know more about?"

Or

"If this is something you like, how much influence do you have in the decision process?"

If they tell you their boss would make the final decision, then, Layer with:

"I understand completely. I'll tell you what, so we don't waste your time or his/hers. Let me have a brief word with him/her, and I will see if this is something he/she even wants to learn more about. I'll be happy to hold on."

If you are then told they aren't available, try to get their name or direct email address or extension, and when you call back, ask for the DM directly.

The major lesson here is that you must resist the temptation to pitch the gatekeeper, or to give too much of your pitch to the assistant if he or she is not the final DM. Give just enough to qualify for interest, and then try to get through to the actual DM. This will save you a lot of time and headache later.

WHAT TO DO IF THE PROSPECT TAKES ONLY EMAILS

I received an email from a reader who said that he sometimes gets the objection from the gatekeeper of, "I am sorry, but he/she does not take outside calls. He/she responds only to emails." He asked if there is a way to get around this, and my answer is, "Sometimes." Let's start at the beginning.

First, my question to the sales rep who sent me this email would be, "How did the gatekeeper know you were an 'outside' call rather than a client, prospect, or someone with a preexisting relationship?" The first thing a sales rep needs to do when prospecting is to use the "please, please, please" technique that I have written about earlier and to be as assumptive, yet polite, as possible. This generally eliminates 60 to 80 percent of the screening you are likely to get.

If you still get the screening of "What's this call in regard to?," once again, you need to use the assumptive, direct approach combined with a second "please" at the end. Something like, "Yes, please tell her it's about her [lead processing], and I'll be happy to hold, please." This will work in most instances. Once again, you must use the openings as I recommend them to avoid most screening to begin with.

If you have used both openings and still get the objection, "She responds only to email," then you can try the following statements, which may sometimes work.

Prospect takes only email—Response 1:

"I *have* emailed in the past, and I think they may be getting stuck in her spam folder. Could you please tell her I need just a minute to confirm this, please?"

Prospect takes only email—Response 2:

"I'd love to email her my information, but I'm not sure which brochure to send. Would you mind if I had just a two-minute conversation to see what would be appropriate, please? I'll be happy to hold."

Prospect takes only email—Response 3:

"And how do I reach her if I don't hear back from my email?"

Prospect takes only email—Response 4:

"I understand, but this is important. May I speak with her supervisor/assistant, please?"

Prospect takes only email—Response 5:

"I understand she may be busy. Who is her manager, please?"

Then:

"Could you please connect me with _____, please?"

Prospect takes only email—Response 6:

"I know what that's like. We have a similar policy here as well, but after three email attempts, the caller is to be put through. Could you tell her I'm holding, please?"

Prospect takes only email—Response 7:

"Question for you: If I haven't heard back from my previous emails, how would *you* recommend I reach her?"

Prospect takes only email—Response 8:

"If I end up not being able to reach her, who *can* you connect me to?"

Prospect takes only email—Response 9:

"My email is down right now. Would you mind putting me through for a quick question?"

Prospect takes only email—Response 10:

"Could I please speak to *your* supervisor, please?"

Prospect takes only email—Response 11:

"What happened the last time you put someone through to her?"

Prospect takes only email—Response 12:

"I'm not allowed to email anyone I don't already have in my database. Would you mind letting her know I'm holding, please?"

Prospect takes only email—Response 13:

"Who *can* you put me through to?"

Prospect takes only email—Response 14:

"Could I have customer service, please?"

(Then just go through them to be put through to your prospect.)

Prospect takes only email—Response 15:

"What would you recommend is the best way to reach her by phone?"

Prospect takes only email—Response 16:

"No problem. For the next time, what is her extension, please?"

These are a variety of responses you can use to get past the gate-keeper and on to your decision maker. Pick the ones that work best for your sale and your personality. If you find that you absolutely cannot get through, try reaching out to your prospect through LinkedIn or other social media.

If you exhaust all of these options and still find you can't get through to a prospect, then consider them disqualified for your product or service and move on. There are plenty of other prospects/deals awaiting your call.

CHAPTER 3

Dealing with Resistance When Prospecting

How to Overcome Initial Resistance While Cold Calling

Many sales reps ask me how to deal with objections when they are prospecting, and they are surprised when I tell them that there are no objections when cold calling. "What do you mean?" they ask. "I get the objections like 'I'm not interested,' and 'I'm too busy,'" and 'We are all set,'" and many others, they tell me. Those are not objections, I counter; those are simply initial resistance statements. I tell them that they use them all time themselves. Think about walking into a department store and being approached by a sales associate, I say. When they ask how they can help you, don't you reply, "I'm just looking?" That is not an objection; rather, it is simply your immediate reaction to someone trying to sell you something.

It's the same thing with your prospects. They get approached all the time, and they also have developed initial resistance statements to blow sales reps off. The reason these are not objections is because your prospect hasn't been pitched anything yet. Because they don't know what you are selling, nor the details of your offering, they can't be objecting yet. Instead, they are just trying to blow you off. The difference here might seem subtle, but it makes a huge difference in how you handle it.

How you handle an initial resistance statement on a prospecting call (and sometimes even close, for that matter) versus how you handle an objection makes a huge difference in terms of how successful you will be. The crucial difference is this: with an objection, your goal is to isolate it so you understand exactly what it is, then handle it with a proven, scripted approach, then confirm it, and then ask for the sale. With an initial resistance statement, however, your goal is not to try to deal with or overcome it. Instead, your goal is to briefly acknowledge it, and then move past it and back into your qualifying. The key here is that you don't buy into the resistance statement and get stuck in trying to overcome it. Remember, you haven't pitched anything yet, so you do not have anything to defend or overcome.

Once you learn to resist the temptation to overcome resistance statements, your cold calling and qualifying job becomes much easier. Once you form the habit of quickly acknowledging a prospect's initial resistance and then moving back into asking questions to engage and qualify your prospect, that is when you stop struggling and pushing against people. More important, once you get better at bypassing someone's initial resistance statements, that is when you get deeper into conversations with prospects, and that's when you begin doing what 80 percent of your competition doesn't do—discover qualified candidates.

All the initial resistance responses you will read in the following section teach you to do just that—briefly acknowledge and then move past the resistance and back into qualifying a prospect. By using the techniques outlined here, you will be able to move past your prospect's initial resistance, past their automatic defense, and into a real conversation to uncover their true needs. The key is that you must be persistent. You must make several attempts to overcome resistance before you give up.

Now, obviously, you won't always be able to get around a prospect's resistance, and sometimes you may determine that someone really isn't interested or a good fit for you at this time. How will you know when to stop? I say give a prospect three rebuttals, and if they still aren't interested in engaging, then let them go. At least you've seriously tried to get past their initial resistance, and you'll be free to move on to the next prospect without wondering if they were just blowing you off or if they really weren't in the market right now.

As with all the scripts and techniques in this book, these initial resistance statements will take practice to perfect. After you read them, take some time to customize your favorites so they fit what you are selling and your personality. Use them repeatedly until you form the new habit of acknowledging initial resistance and moving back into a qualifying question rather than fighting, challenging, or trying to overcome an objection. If you do this, you will keep control of the sales process, and you will get deeper and deeper into conversations with actual buyers.

EIGHTEEN NEW WAYS TO HANDLE "I'M NOT INTERESTED"

Regardless of what kind of prospecting you're doing—whether you are calling back in-bound leads who have contacted you, or old accounts who haven't purchased in a while, or just straight cold calls—you are still going to get a good dose of the blow-off resistance statement "I'm not interested." While I have provided many ways of handling this in the past, here are 18 new, customized responses for each of the lead categories from before.

"I'm Not Interested"

For "Warm" Leads Who Have Filled Out an Online Form or Reached Out in Some Way

I'm not interested—Response 1:

> "That's perfectly okay, _____, you've probably forgotten that you (filled in a form, requested info, and so forth) so I don't expect you to be interested in what you must think is a cold call. But just to remind you—on [date/time] you [visited our website/dropped by our booth/filled out a form, and so forth]. Do you remember that?"

> (If yes)

> "What did you need at that time?"

> (Listen carefully)

> I'm not interested—Response 2:

> "No problem, _____. I also forget half the things I request info on! Just to remind you, we [what you do], and on [date/time] you [visited our website/dropped by our booth/filled out a form, and so forth] Do you remember that?"

(If yes)

"Do you remember what prompted you to reach out to us at that time?"

I'm not interested—Response 3:

"That's fine; quick question though: When you filled out [our online form, and so forth] has anyone else from our office contacted you about it yet?"

(If no)

"I see. Well, I do apologize for that. Just out of curiosity, did you get that handled yet, or are you still looking?"

For Inactive Accounts or People You've Not Spoken to in a While

I'm not interested—Response 1:

"That's fine, _____. I'm simply calling to update your account information for our records. Quick question: Are you still the right contact person who handles ordering the _____ for your company?"

I'm not interested—Response 2:

"Oh, that's okay. I'm not calling to sell you anything today. I just want to make sure you still know we're here in case you do need something down the road. By the way, do you guys still carry/use/order _____?"

I'm not interested—Response 3:

"I get that all the time, and just to let you know the only reason I'm calling is to introduce myself as your contact, should you ever need to check pricing or availability on an item. Quick question: Are you still the right contact for _____?"

I'm not interested—Response 4:

"No problem, _____. I'll simply email you my contact information in case you ever do need anything, and then I'll get out of your hair. By the way, would you be the best person to email this to, or is there someone else who is handling _____ now?"

I'm not interested—Response 5:

"That's no problem at all. A quick question: Is it that you don't need any-thing just now, or do you even order/carry _____ any more at all?"

(If they say "We do order. We just don't need any now.")

"Great. When you are in the market again, could I be one of the [ven-dors/suppliers/sources] you go to for a quote?"

For Cold Calling or Prospecting Calls

I'm not interested—Response 1:

"Quick question: Does that mean you're not interested at this moment, but in a few months, things could change, and I should keep in touch?"

I'm not interested—Response 2:

"Who else at your company do you think might have a need for something like this?"

I'm not interested—Response 3:

"I'm with you. A quick question though: Are you the right contact for this, or is there another department (or person) I should check with?"

I'm not interested—Response 4:

"When should I check back with you?"

(If given a date)

"Great. So I can be more prepared for that, I have just a quick question: Are you the right contact for this?"

(If they seem open, then add other qualifying questions.)

I'm not interested—Response 5:

"If you were to be interested, what is the typical [volume, amount, fre-quency, and so on] that you normally order/use/need?"

(If they tell you)

"And who do you normally get that from?"

I'm not interested—Response 6:

"When was the last time you *were* interested in something like this?"

I'm not interested—Response 7:

"And what would have to change for you to be more open to something like this in the future?"

I'm not interested—Response 8:

"Should I lose your number or put you on a six-month follow-up call?"

(Say this with a *big* smile in your voice! If they say call back in six months, then say the following.)

"Great. What should I keep an eye out for in between, now and then?"

I'm not interested—Response 9:

"The next time you are interested in [your product], could I get back with you and see if we can help?"

(If yes)

"When should I follow up with you?"

I'm not interested—Response 10:

"Thanks for letting me know up front. If I were to get back with you in the future, what would I have to have to get you to be more open to something like this?"

So there you have it: 18 more ways of handling the "I'm not interested" objection.

As always, make sure to customize these responses to fit your product or service and to fit your personality. Once you find one that feels right, and that gets your prospects to open up, then stick with it and practice it over and over again. Remember: practice of the right responses will always make perfect.

FIVE NEW WAYS TO HANDLE "JUST EMAIL ME SOMETHING"

The method of this stall has changed throughout the years. It went from, "Just put a brochure in the mail, and I'll look at it," to "Why don't you fax something to me, and I'll look it over," to "Just email me your information." Unfortunately, it all still means the same thing: your prospect either doesn't want to take the time to be pitched, or they don't need what you are selling.

Either way, this stall sets up one of the most frustrating parts of sales—the chase. Think about it: How many times have you sent off your information and, when you've been fortunate enough to "catch" the prospect again, you've heard: "I haven't looked at it" or "We're not interested at this time"? Probably a lot, right?

The way to avoid this is to earn the right to ask a few key qualifying (or disqualifying, as I like to call them) questions so you can save both of you a lot of time and effort later (to say nothing of saving yourself a lot of disappointment as well).

The solution, as always, is to be prepared for this brush-off with a good script that fits your personality and product or service. Take the time now to adapt and customize two or more of the following responses so you are prepared the next time your prospect uses this stall.

"Just Email Me Something"

Just email me something—Response 1:

> "I'll be happy to do that, but once you see the material, you will probably have more questions than answers, so let's do this first: I'll ask you just a couple of *quick* questions to see if this is even a fit for you at this time, and then, if it is, I'll send you some targeted information. Sound fair?"

> (If yes, ask any of the following questions.)

> "First, would you be the right contact for handling (Software, training…)?"

> *Or*

> "I know I called you out of the blue, but if you found that you could [give a benefit of your product or service], what might your time frame be for considering doing something with it?"

Or

"How are you currently handling (training, software, and so on), and what might motivate you to consider making a change?"

Or

"How open are you to seriously considering making a change (or making a move on) (training, software, and so on) in the next one or two months?"

Just email me something—Response 2:

"You bet I can—what's your email address?"

[Take it down and then email them your information right then!]

"Okay, I just sent it. Now while you open that up, let me ask you a quick question: "How do you get involved in ordering/handling/working with the (training, software, and so on)?"

Or

"From a needs standpoint, how motivated is [your company/department /are you] to change/fix/replace/buy Software right now?"

Or

"What would you need to see in the information I just sent you for you to become interested in learning more about what we do?"

Just email me something—Response 3:

"I'd be more than happy to do that—where should I email that to?"

(Take it down and then email them your information right then.)

"Okay. It's on the way to you. What I'd like to do right now is take just two minutes to get an idea of what's important to you, and then I can direct you to that part of the information when you get around to it. Let me ask you:

"How do you get involved in ordering/handling/working with the (supplies, leads, etc.)?"

Or

"From a needs standpoint, how motivated is [your company/department/ are you] to change/fix/replace/buy training right now?"

Or

"What would you need to see in the information I just sent you for you to become seriously interested in making a change in how you're handling (training, software, and so on) now?"

Just email me something—Response 4:

"I have a better idea. Rather than send you something you may not be really interested in, I'll save you the time of going through it—or deleting it—by asking you just a couple of quick questions now to see if there's really a need. If there is, then I'll have my assistant email you something."

"Are you the best person to talk to about changing/replacing/ordering the (training, software, and so on)?"

Or

"I know I called you out of the blue, but if you found that you could [give a benefit of your product or service], what might your time frame be for considering making a decision on it?"

Or

"How are you currently handling (training, software, and so on), and what might motivate you to consider making a change?"

Or

"How open are you too seriously considering making a change (or making a move on) (training, software, and so on) in the next one to two months?"

Just email me something—Response 5

"I would be happy to do that—where do you want me to email that to?"

(Then)

"And while you have me on the phone, let me briefly ask you just a couple of quick questions that will determine whether it makes sense for me to follow up on the information I'll send you. For example:

"How likely are you [or your company/department] to be in the market to make a change in (the way you handle (training, software, and so on)) if you found a better alternative?"

Or

"If you like what you see in the information, what would the next step for us be?"

Or

"What would realistically stand in the way of us doing business together in the next few weeks if you saw some value in the information?"

There you have it—five new ways to handle the age-old brush-off, "Just mail/fax/email me some information." As will all new scripts, take some time to adapt them to fit your product or service, and to fit your personality and style. Once you do develop an effective way of delivering this information, then commit to practicing, drilling, and rehearsing it until it becomes automatic for you.

FIVE (NINE, REALLY!) NEW WAYS TO HANDLE "I'M TOO BUSY"

Of all the brush-offs you get while prospecting, the good old standby: "I'm too busy to talk now," is right up there with, "I'm not interested," and "Just email me something." The reason this is such a popular response with prospects is that most salespeople don't know how to handle it and are easily put off and happy to "call back later." Of course, this is just what the prospect wants them to do, and, since they now have your caller ID number, they will know to let the call go to voice mail the next time they see it!

The key to handling this stall—as with all others—is to bypass it first and earn the right to ask a few, quick qualifying questions to see if you are dealing with a qualified buyer or not.

That is what the following rebuttals allow you to do.

As with any brush-off, objection, or stall, though, this one is easy to handle if you just take the time to learn some proven responses to it, and then use them with confidence when you get it.

To help you deal with this brush-off more effectively, I urge you to pick any of the following responses that best suits your style, product, and service. Feel free to change them slightly so they are most comfortable for you to use, and then practice them every time you encounter this initial blow-off. Here they are.

"I'm Too Busy"

I'm too busy—Response 1:

"I completely understand, and I know what it's like to be interrupted. Tell you what: before I schedule a call back with you, let's take just a moment now to make sure this is something that's even worth it for me to call you back about.

"Quick question: How open are you to considering a new vendor to handle your [product or service], if you found you could realistically save yourself time and money?"

Or

"Quick question: We supply/have a solution for/provide [your product or service], and the clients who schedule a 10-minute call with us are really happy they learned about it. I'm willing to call you back later today or even tomorrow morning, but first: What would you say your level of interest would be in making a move to a more efficient way of [doing what your product or service does]?"

I'm too busy—Response 2:

"I'm with you, and let's face it—we're all too busy until we hear about something that can really benefit us. Let me tell you in a nutshell how this can help you, and then if you'd like to know more, we can schedule a time that's better later. Fair enough?"

(If yes, then *briefly* give a description and use a qualifying tie-down question.)

I'm too busy—Response 3:

"Got it, and I won't keep you. Quick question: Are you the right person to speak with in regard to [your product or service]?"

(If yes)

"Great, then before I schedule a time to get back with you, let me just ask you two quick things: Number one, if you found that you could increase [list a benefit or two], and reduce your [again, list a benefit or two], how open would you be to viewing a demo on it?"

(Let them answer.)

"And two, if you decided this was worthy enough to seriously consider, who, besides yourself, would weigh in on making that decision?"

"Great, then let's go ahead and schedule that. I've got two times tomorrow...."

I'm too busy—Response 4:

"Wow, you *do* sound busy! No worries—I can either call you back in 20 minutes, or we can spend just two minutes now to see if this is a fit for you. If not, then I won't have to bother you again. How does that sound?"

Or

"Yes, you do sound busy. Okay, would you like me to call you back in an hour or later this afternoon?"

Or

"Okay, no problem. Let me see.... well, I could call you back this afternoon, or we could set up a brief five-minute call tomorrow morning. Which works best for you?"

I'm too busy—Response 5:

"Hey, I know what it's like to be busy—but the last thing I want to do is schedule a call back if you're really not interested in what I've got, so let's do this: I'll ask you just a quick question or two and if there's some interest on your end, then we'll schedule some time later. Fair enough?

(If yes)

"Great. _____, are you open to purchasing/investing/learning about a new way to handle your [your product] if you were convinced it would save you time/make your job easier/be better at....?"

Or

"Quickly, what would your timeline be for [changing/investing/trying] a new service for your [what your product or service does] if you found you could dramatically increase/save, and so forth?"

Once again, remember that your job is to bypass initial resistance and earn the right to ask a few qualifying questions to see if your prospect is even worth putting on your call-back list. By using the preceding scripts, you will be able to do just that.

FIVE NEW WAYS TO HANDLE "WE'RE CURRENTLY WORKING WITH SOMEONE"

If you are selling one of the more popular products or services on the market (and who isn't?), then you probably run into this blow-off all the time. Like most brush-offs, prospects like to use this because it works—unprepared reps usually respond with a feeble: "Oh, okay, well, could I call you back in six months?"

Being prepared with a few good scripts will allow you to get past this objection, and will allow you to qualify an opportunity that most other people would miss. As always, I advise you to customize the following scripts to fit your personality, product, or service, and then to practice them repeatedly until they become automatic.

"We're Currently Working with Someone Else"

We're currently working with someone—Response 1:

"No problem at all. While I have you on the phone, what I'd recommend you do is at least learn about a few features we offer that you may not be getting now, so if you ever need to reach out to another company, at least you'll have an idea of what's out there. In fact, let me ask you: Are you getting [something you offer that your competition doesn't]?"

We're currently working with someone—Response #2:

"That's great, and let me ask you: If in two minutes I can give you an idea of why more companies are switching to us, would you at least accept an email with my contact information for when you do need to consider using someone else?"

(If yes)

"Great—the number one reason companies switch to us is for [price, service, value]. Are you currently getting that now?"

We're currently working with someone—Response 3:

"Who are you using?"

(Wait to hear, then say the following.)

"That's a good company. In fact, they are the reason that we created our [name your advantage]. It's something that takes what they do, but makes it better. Have you heard about it?"

(Listen for an opening.)

"If you're interested, I can show you two or three other things we do differently, and then you can judge for yourself if you'd like to learn more. Fair enough?"

We're currently working with someone—Response 4:

"That's great. It means you are in our sweet spot. For the future, though, you might want to know that in addition to the [product/service] you're getting from them, we can also give you price, service, value. Would you find that useful?"

We're currently working with someone—Response 5:

"That's great—because things change so quickly in this market, it means that we can be a great resource for you for when you need to compare pricing or services down the line. Let me quickly ask you:

"Are you the best contact for this?"

Or

"How did you decide to use [the other company] for this?"

Or

"What do you wish they did better?"

Or

"How open would you be if we could show you how to do (improve, save time, etc.)?"

These scripts are designed to start a dialogue with someone and get past their initial reflex response. If you can get someone talking to you, you have a much better chance to find an opening and create an opportunity to uncover a qualified lead.

TEN NEW WAYS TO HANDLE "WE'RE ALL SET"

I receive emails from my readers all the time asking me how to handle various objections and resistance statements. A common request I get is how to handle the initial resistance statement "We're all set." A variation of this is anything along the lines of:

"We are okay with our present system."

Or

"We've already got a company that handles that."

Or

"We're fine for right now."

As you can see, these are all basically the same, and, more important, they aren't objections—rather, they are still initial resistance statements or blow-offs. Essentially, they are saying something along the lines of: "I'm not interested in being pitched right now. Please go away."

The key to handling resistance, remember, is not to try to overcome it (remember, it's not an objection) but rather to simply bypass it and get into your pitch. So with that in mind, here's how you handle the "We're all set" blow-off and any of its variations:

"We're All Set"

We're all set—Response 1:

"That's great, and I'd just like to see if we could get on your vendor list for the next time you're in the market. Let me ask you...."

Now get into your qualifying questions.

We're all set—Response 2:

"Most companies I speak with are 'all set' and that's why I'm reaching out to you now. I want to give you an option for the next time you're in need of this. Let me ask you...."

Back to qualifying.

We're all set—Response 3:

"No problem. Let me ask you: The next time you need this, what is number one on your wish list?"

We're all set—Response 4:

"I understand—I didn't expect to catch you in the market right now. Instead, let me get an idea of your perfect profile, and then I'll send you some information you can keep on file next time you need this...."

Now re engage by asking a qualifying question.

We're all set—Response 5:

"Got it. Let me ask you: The next time you need this, are you the right person to speak to about it?"

If yes, then qualify them for that next time—especially asking about time frame, budget, and any other qualifiers you can.

We're all set—Response 6:

"I understand, and let me ask you: When is your next buying season for this?"

Then keep the conversation going by asking additional qualifying questions.

We're all set—Response 7:

"That's fine. I totally understand. And let me ask you: The next time you are in the market for this, how many companies are you going to reach out to?"

Then ask how you can become one of them, what their budget is, who the decision makers are, and so forth.

We're all set—Response 8:

"No problem. What you might find helpful is to know about our special pricing and the additional services we provide. Did you know that ... "

Then pitch one or two things you do that others don't—and use a tie-down!

We're all set—Response 9:

"I'm glad you said that. What I've found is that those companies that are already using a vendor for this are surprised to learn that ... "

Give them a shocking statement about how you have just been rated number one, or that you give free delivery, or another outstanding value statement; something that will pique their interest.

We're all set—Response 10:

"No problem. Could I be the next company in line the next time you are in the market for this?"

(If yes),

"Great, let me get your email and send you my info...."

Then:

"And just out of curiosity, what would have to change for you to even begin looking at someone else?"

Look for an opening here to qualify the prospect.

So there you have it—10 new ways of handling this age-old blow-off. Just remember, your goal is not to try to overcome this—rather, it is to bypass this resistance statement and get information you can use to create value and continue the conversation.

How to Overcome "We Handle That in House"

If you are trying to set appointments for an outside sales team, or even if you are trying to generate leads so you can do an over-the-phone demo later, then many of the stalls we have discussed so far are probably very familiar to you. While we have already discussed common initial resistance statements like, "I'm not interested" and "Just email me something," there are others that seem somewhat harder to overcome. One of the more frequently encountered statements is "We handle that in house, so we don't need you."

Many sales reps are taught the normal, old-school approaches like:

"That's fine, but when was the last time you did an apples-to-apples comparison to what it might run you if you outsourced that?"

Or

"But if I could show you a way to save money, then surely you'd want to know more about it, wouldn't you?"

While either of these responses can be used effectively in the right situation, there is a better way to handle this objection. What you want to do is offer value in your visit or demo, and then leave it up to your prospect to decide if it is worth taking your call or visit any further.

Try the following rebuttal (obviously, customize this to your particular service or product) to the objection "We handle that in house":

"That's fine—glad you have a way that's working for you now. Here's what I'd recommend you do though: I'd be happy to drop by and show you how we'd go about taking care of that for you, and what our processes look like.

"At the end, you may still choose to keep doing it the way you are, but at least you will have a different perspective on it, and you may even find some ways to save even more money or time. The visit wouldn't take long, and everyone we meet with finds a benefit.

"What is a good time for you next week?"

As you can see here, you are not pitching, necessarily; you are instead offering to show them a better way. What they do after that is up to them.

Try using this for the next couple of weeks and see if you can get past a prospect's natural resistance to setting up a meeting. This approach can also be adapted if you are just setting up a demo over the phone rather than setting up an appointment. If you use it consistently, you are going to set more appointments, open more doors, and close more sales.

HOW TO HANDLE THE "WE'RE HAPPY WITH STATUS QUO" OBJECTION

As you know, I often get emails from readers of my e-zine, *Secrets of the Top 20 Percent*, asking me how I would handle various selling situations and objections. (If you have not signed up yet, you can do so for free on my homepage: www.mrinsidesales.com. By doing so, you will get new, word-for-word scripts each Tuesday.)

A reader recently sent in a request asking me how to deal with the "We are used to the status quo and don't want to make waves" objection. This reader also wrote that he had been told by another training company that he needed to "make them painfully aware of something they don't see coming (like a freight train) and develop a more compelling message." As you might imagine, he wasn't able to come up with anything that was working.

By the way, I must comment here that I frequently hear this about other "sales training" companies: they are quick to offer what sounds like good advice, but they then do not provide the specific solutions to back it up. As you know from reading my e-zines, watching my YouTube videos, or reading or listening to my books and CDs, I not only tell you *what* to do, but also *how* to do it.

In this case, I think the reader was having trouble with this technique because, to begin with, it's not a good approach. Trying to convince someone that what they are doing now is a bad idea and that it is going to lead to big trouble (so you can say, "I told you so" later) isn't going to endear you to anyone. What I recommend instead is to find a way to bypass this obvious initial resistance statement and find a way to present your product or service in a nonthreatening way.

Your goal on the prospecting call is not to overcome objections (which this isn't, by the way), but rather, to qualify and set a date up to demo your product or service. Here are some sample scripts to help you do just that.

"We're happy with Status Quo"

Status quo—Rebuttal 1:

"I'm completely with you and believe me, I don't want to rock the boat. But because things change all the time, there might come a time when you need to consider your options. So let's do this: I'll set a time to give you a brief demo of what we do and how it might help you. After we do, you can then decide if you want to do anything with it now, or keep it in your back pocket in case you ever need to consider a different source. Sound good?"

Status quo—Rebuttal 2:

"I understand, and I'll try not to make too many waves here. Just out of curiosity, when was the last time you did compare services and pricing—you know, just to keep current on what's available to you?"

Status quo—Rebuttal 3:

"I'm with you, and believe me, I'm not here to cause trouble. But let me ask you this: Isn't it wise to at least know about your options just in case you need to make a change at some time in the future?"

Status quo—Rebuttal 4:

"I'm with you. So tell you what: instead of me trying to sell you something, let me just educate you on what is currently available in the marketplace. You know, so in case you need something further down the line, you will know whom to call. Make sense?"

Status quo—Rebuttal 5:

"No problem, I fully understand. Let me ask you this though: If something were to happen to your current provider, wouldn't you at least want a dependable backup plan so you didn't miss a beat?"

The point of these rebuttals is to bypass this resistance so you can get in front of a qualified lead and pitch your product or service. Obviously, once they agree to do a demo with you, you will want to ask other qualifying questions. As always, I encourage you to practice, drill, and rehearse your responses so you can internalize them and deliver them in a natural-sounding way.

CHAPTER 4

You Can't Sell an Unqualified Lead

Qualifying Scripts to Identify Real Buyers

A s I said in the beginning, cold calling (or prospecting) and learning how to properly qualify your prospects and customers is *the* most important skill you can master in sales. Knowing how to identify who is a real candidate for your product or service, versus who is just looking, or worse, who is just accepting your information to get you off the phone, makes the difference between closing sales and pitching unqualified leads who never buy.

Unfortunately, qualifying skills are rarely taught in sales today. Instead, most sales teams are encouraged to fill their pipeline and then hope for the best. Years ago, when I was among a sales team of 25 other securities brokers, we were taught the same thing—to fill our pipeline. Our sales manager at the time used to say, "Eight and five to stay alive!" He meant that we needed to generate eight new leads (send out information to prospects to close later) and conduct five presentations per day to make our revenue numbers. This turned out to be not only exhausting, but ineffective, as well. Worse, it encouraged us to do a lousy job of qualifying prospects, as our goal wasn't to find interested buyers. It was rather to send out a bunch of "leads" so we had a bunch of prospects to pitch later.

What the team—myself included—ended up doing was sending out brochures to anyone who would take them, and then calling back and hoping for the best. "Throw as much crap on the wall as you can, and some of it will stick," was the philosophy. Well, that stunk! Calling back and chasing 20 or 30 leads or more, hoping someone would listen, and then, after an hour of pitching, finally buy was a terrible way to do sales. Ending the day and week frustrated wasn't much fun. Everything changed for me, though, once I finally committed to learning how to qualify my leads.

The first thing that happened was that I became unwilling to just send out brochures to anyone who would take one. Instead, I developed a qualifying checklist (very much like the one I talked about earlier on), and if a prospect wasn't willing to answer most of my questions, then I didn't send them information and put them in my pipeline. By developing stringent criteria as to who I would spend time with and who I wouldn't, my lead numbers went down drastically. Instead of getting eight leads out per day, I went down to eight in a week! My sales manager was appalled, and quite concerned. I wasn't.

The reason I wasn't worried was that out of eight really qualified leads, I began closing five of them. Suddenly, I had the best closing percentage in the office, and because I wasn't sending out unqualified leads any longer, I had a lot more time to prospect and find more qualified buyers. I got to spend my time cold calling and looking for qualified prospects rather than wasting my time trying to do the impossible: close unqualified leads.

My sales manager soon got off my back as my close rate went through the roof and as my sales revenue began to surpass most of the others in the office. My confidence went up as well, because I no longer spent time with unqualified leads. In fact, I developed the philosophy of "disqualifying" rather than qualifying leads. I now had a rule that prospects needed to earn the right to go into my pipeline. Because so many more deals were coming out of my pipeline, I changed the analogy from a funnel or pipeline to a "sales cylinder." I was soon closing almost as many leads as I was putting in.

And it all started when I learned how to properly qualify a lead. I learned how to ask the tough questions and how to really listen to my prospect's answers. I got honest with myself and asked if I would be excited about calling a certain prospect back? If not, then I kept qualifying. If I heard red flags, then I used "layering" questions to get to the truth. If I determined that someone wasn't ready to buy—for whatever reason—or if I determined that there were too many objections standing in the way, then I wouldn't send my information. Instead, I picked up the phone and moved on. "Next" became my rallying cry. "Some will; some won't. Who's next?" is what I repeatedly told myself. I finally found that I didn't need the practice of pitching unqualified leads. Rather, I needed the practice of finding and qualifying motivated prospects, so that is where I spent most of my time.

I present to you in the next section the advanced course of qualifying sales prospects. You will find word-for-word questions on how to discover what a prospect's budget is, how truly interested they are, and how to handle influencers. You will also learn how to requalify prospects and customers, and you will learn what the two most important qualifiers are and how to ask for them. By mastering the art of qualifying prospects and customers, you will take your sales career into the upper part of the Top 20 Percent, and that is when sales becomes fun—and easy.

FIFTEEN WAYS TO HANDLE THE COMPETITION OBJECTION

We all face competition. There is always someone who can do something cheaper, or faster, or better (at least in the mind of your prospect). Because of this, prospects—and even customers—are constantly on the search for a better deal. Knowing how to handle the competition objection effectively can mean the difference between winning the sale or suffering that sinking feeling of having lost the business to someone else.

There are several times you can handle the competition objection, but surprisingly, most sales reps wait until it comes up at the end of their closing presentation. This is the worst time to handle it, because you have already given your pricing and options, and sometimes even your best deal. While you may have to handle the objection of competition during the close—and I will give you some scripts to do just that later in this section—the best time to handle it is in the beginning, while qualifying. Here are some ways you can do that.

Qualifying for Competition during the Cold Call

Qualifying for competition during the cold call—Response 1:

"_____, let's talk a little bit about who else you're looking at for this—who's top of your list right now?"

If you are uncomfortable bringing up potential competition, let me assure you of two things: one, if they are shopping you, then they are most likely shopping others, so don't be surprised. Two, trust me, it is better to know in advance who you are up against so you can position yourself to win the business during the close. Always ask this in an assumptive way.

Qualifying for competition during the cold call—Response 2:

"How many companies are you getting quotes on for this?"

Once again, don't worry about introducing the concept of getting quotes, if they are going to do this (and most are), it's better to get an idea of it now. If they tell you they are getting three quotes (doesn't matter how many), layer this with:

"And who have you liked so far?" Again, be assumptive with this, and don't be afraid of an answer. You want to know this in advance.

Qualifying for competition during the cold call—Response 3:

"_____, how does your current supplier fit into all of this?"

This is a nice, open-ended, assumptive way to get your prospect to reveal why they might be moving away from their current vendor—or why they might still be considering using them. A great way to layer this is to ask:

Qualifying for competition during the cold call—Response 4:

"And if you find that we can give you a better deal than you are getting right now, what would you do next?"

Obviously, you want them to reveal that they will take it back to their current vendor to get them to lower their price, and this is what you want to know in advance. Asking this question in an opened-ended way like this often gets them to reveal this. You can also ask this in a more direct way:

Qualifying for competition during the cold call—Response 5:

"_____, if we can show you how we can take care of what you are doing now, and do so for less than you are paying your current vendor, what would prevent you from taking it back to them and getting them to just drop their price to keep your business?"

Listen carefully to not only what your prospect says here, but how they say it. If they hesitate, or if their voice goes up or wavers a bit, then you are in trouble. You can also handle it this way:

Qualifying for competition during the cold call—Response 6:

"Now _____, after we do our analysis I'm pretty convinced that we will be able to save you money just like we do our other clients. But _____, I have a concern and I need you to level with me: sometimes we go through all this work to find these savings, and after we do, some companies use them to get their current vendor to lower their prices. Do you see what I mean?"

(Wait for response.)

"So I'm happy to do the work for you and show you what we can do for you, but let me ask you: What is the chance that you will take this back to your current vendor to see if they will match it?"

Or

"Let me ask you: If we can also show you savings, what would prevent you from asking your current vendor to do the same?"

Qualifying for competition during the cold call—Response 7:

"_____, what is going to be the deciding factor on who wins your business on this?"

And if it's price, then layer with:

"Okay then, after you get all the quotes, will you at least let me compete against the lowest quote to see if I can do better?"

(If yes)

"And if I can beat the price you have, would you then move forward and put me to work for you?"

If, after you have presented your product or service, your prospect says they want or need to check on other offers/estimates/quotes, then use the following questions to get your prospect to open up and possibly reveal what it would take for you to win the business:

Handling Competition during the Close

Handling competition during the close—Question 1:

"I understand. Which way are you leaning right now?"

Handling competition during the close—Question 2:

"What would it take for someone else to win your business?"

Handling competition during the close—Question 3:

"What would it honestly take for you to choose us for this?"

Handling competition during the close—Question 4:

"What don't you see with our proposal that you see in others?"

Handling competition during the close—Question 5:

"Are we in the running with what else you've seen out there?"

(If yes)

"What about us would take us out of the running?"

Or

"What would you need to see to choose us?"

And

"What can I do right now to ensure that we win your business?"

Handling competition during the close—Question 6:

"Obviously, you are going to show this quote to your current vendor—if they match the price, will you just stick with them?"

(If yes)

"What can I do to prevent that?"

Handling competition during the close—Question 7:

"How many times have you taken other quotes to your current vendor?"

(If they tell you):

"And what do they usually do?"

(If they say they lower their price to keep the business.)

"How can we break that cycle and get you the right pricing from the start?"

Handling competition during the close—Question 8:

"_____, let's take your lowest bid right now and compare it—services to services—to what we are offering you. If I find you are getting a better deal, I'll tell you so. If I can beat it, then I'll let you know that as well. Either way—you will win! Do you have that other quote nearby?"

Remember, competition will always exist, but you can beat it and win business *if* you are prepared with proven and effective scripts like those offered to you here. Once again, pick your favorite ones and tailor them to your sale.

You now have a variety of ways to handle the most common initial resistance statements you get when cold calling or prospecting for your product or service. Because there is very little new in the world of sales—most resistance, stalls, and objections are the same, even across industries—arming yourself with proven responses to these stalls will make your cold calling much, much easier. Commit to adapting and practicing these proven responses over and over, and soon your confidence will go up as you get past the initial resistance that used to frustrate you—and that still blows off most of your competition.

HOW TO QUESTION FOR BUDGET

Qualifying for budget, or handling objections around budget and money, are areas most sales reps feel uncomfortable in. To start with, I have heard many sales reps tell me that bringing up budget or money on a qualifying call is not only uncomfortable, but that it's inappropriate as well. They say, "I haven't given any value yet, so it's too early to talk about budget!"

My response is that if your product or service is out of a prospect's budget, or if they feel it is too expensive, then it doesn't matter how much value you give it—most are not going to buy from you. That is why it is crucial to qualify for budget up front—or at the very least about budget range—just as you would with the decision maker, the time frame, and so on.

When objections about money or price come up, again, sales reps often struggle with how to handle it. In fact, most sales reps' default response is to try to lower the price rather than either build value or help the prospect find other areas to get budget from. We will handle these situations later during the closing scripts.

Next, however, you will find a variety of ways of both qualifying for budget and asking questions to help assist you in helping the prospect uncover potential areas to free up the budget. Getting comfortable with regularly asking these questions—both during the qualifying stage and during the close—will allow you to both identify qualified prospects and help you close them.

As always, adapt them to fit your product, service, or personality and then practice, drill, and rehearse them until they become automatic for you.

Budget Questions during Qualifying

Budget questions during qualifying—Question 1:

"How much budget do you have set aside for new advertising [or this week, quarter, or year]?"

Budget questions during qualifying—Question 2:

"How much are you currently spending to attract new consumers?"

Budget questions during qualifying—Question 3:

"How much budget do you currently spend on keeping or retaining your existing customers?"

Budget questions during qualifying—Question 4:

"How much have you set aside [for your product or service]?"

Budget questions during qualifying—Question 5:

"What do you know about management's budget when it comes to adding [your product or service]?"

Budget questions during qualifying—Question 6:

"Besides yourself, who else would weigh in on making a budget decision on this?"

Layer:

"And what is their role [or your role] in that process?"

Layer:

"And what do you know about their budget for adding a new.... [your product or service]"

Budget questions during qualifying—Question 7:

"How much of a priority is this [your product or service area] for you this month (or quarter)?"

Budget questions during qualifying—Question 8:

"How much does your department [or company] spend on new client acquisition?"

Budget questions during qualifying—Question 9:

"Our solution runs a ballpark of $10,000 up to $50,000. If you liked what you saw, could you work within that range?"

Budget questions during qualifying—Question 10:

"What is your budget for this?"

Budget questions during qualifying—Question 11:

"What are your plans for [your product or service area] for the upcoming season/quarter for this?"

Budget Questions during the Close

Budget questions during the close—Question 1:

"What is a new customer worth, roughly, to you?"

Layer:

"And how much budget, per week/month/year, have you set aside to attract those new customers?"

Layer:

"And how much of that budget is still not used that you could apply to this?"

Budget questions during the close—Question 2:

"When something like this comes up that you believe will work for you [your department or company], how do you normally go about getting the budget for it?"

Budget questions during the close—Question 3:

"How do you draw from next month's/quarter's budget to get something like this that you really know will help you now?"

Budget questions during the close—Question 4:

"What is your yearly budget for this area [of your product or service]"

Layer:

"And how much of that do you have left over?"

Budget questions during the close—Question 5:

"Let me ask you: Around this time of year, how do you handle these kinds of purchases?"

Budget questions during the close—Question 6:

"Who else could you get approval from to afford this extra expense?"

Budget questions during the close—Question 7:

"How do you normally get something above budget approved?"

Budget questions during the close—Question 8:

"How can you borrow against next year's budget to get the profits and results this year?"

Budget questions during the close—Question 9:

"What do you have to do now to make sure this is properly budgeted for next quarter?"

Budget questions during the close—Question 10:

"What other areas/departments can you borrow from to start this service today?"

Budget questions during the close—Question 11:

"If money were not an issue here, would you move forward?"

(If yes)

"*Great!* What are three ways you can think of right now to get the budget for this?"

Budget questions during the close—Question 12:

"What did you do the last time you really wanted something?"

Budget questions during the close—Question 13:

"How did you get the money the last time you really wanted something?"

Budget questions during the close—Question 14:

"We all have ways of getting the money when we really want something. What way do you have of getting the money now?"

Budget questions during the close—Question 15:

"Who [which department] could you borrow from?"

Budget questions during the close—Question 16:

"How about I put you on our low-cost down payment program, and you can then set up easy monthly payments so you can get started today?"

As you can see, there are a variety of ways of not only bringing up or getting clarity around the budget issue, but of also leading your prospect to reveal how and when he or she can get or find the budget. Have some fun with these questions and hit mute while you get all the answers and solutions around budget that you need to close the sale!

How to Qualify for Interest

Today it seems to be harder and harder for sales reps to qualify for genuine interest and to identify buying motives. One thing making this so difficult is the decision tree: there are often many different levels of decision makers (influencers, vetting committees, CEOs, regional managers, corporate, and so on), and sales reps often just skip any attempt to qualify for interest.

Instead, they just send their information or schedule their demo and hope for the best.

As you might suspect, the way around this is to be prepared with scripted questions that are assumptive in nature and that are designed to lead your prospect into revealing what the buying motives (or motivation in general) are for the various other departments and decision makers. Knowing, and thus being able to navigate, the sometimes-convoluted decision tree and tracing the shared buying motivation can be the key to persevering and winning the sale.

Use the following scripts (or customize them to fit your product or service), so you can gain an understanding of what the buying motives are and how to tailor your pitch to each group to close the sale.

Questions to Qualify for Interest

Qualifying for interest—Question 1:

"_____, why did you [or corporate/manager/boss] choose the solution you're using now?"

Layer:

"And what are you [they] looking to improve upon now?"

Qualifying for interest—Question 2:

"If you were to pick one thing that would be a deal killer if it weren't there, what would it be?"

Qualifying for interest—Question 3:

"What have you heard they are [corporate, their manager, boss, and so on] specifically looking for in the next [your product or service]?"

Qualifying for interest—Question 4:

"Besides price, what else is important to [you, them, and so forth]?"

Qualifying for interest—Question 5:

"I know that this [your solution] may seem to be all the same, but tell me, what will stand out for you? What's the one or two things you are really hoping to see?"

Qualifying for interest—Question 6:

"_____, what have you heard in terms of what the priorities are for adding this [your product/service]?

Layer:

"And what is the time frame you are hearing for implementation?"

Qualifying for interest—Question 7:

"Out of all the companies you have [or corporate/manager/boss] seen so far, what looks the best to you?"

Layer:

"And why is that?"

Qualifying for interest—Question 8:

"If you had to pick one thing that this is going to come down to—you know, one thing that you think will be the deciding factor as to who you [corporate/manager/boss] will choose, what do you think that will be?"

Layer:

"Besides price [or whatever they say] , what's next?"

Qualifying for interest—Question 9:

"_____, you haven't made a change so far, just out of curiosity, what is motivating you to consider doing so now?"

Qualifying for interest—Question 10:

"_____, I know I called you out of the blue. I'm glad you are interested in seeing what we have. I have a quick question for you, though: What do you think it will take to persuade the [corporate/manager/boss] to move on something like this?"

I bet you can think of some of your own, can't you? Always remember that your prospect has all the answers as to why they will choose a particular solution. The key to any sale is getting your prospect to tell you what those reasons or buying motives are. If you can do that, you'll make your job much, much easier.

How to Qualify an Influencer

If this were a perfect world, then while prospecting and qualifying we would always get to speak with the decision maker. And while qualifying them, we would discover exactly what they were looking for in a product or solution, and we would also discover that they had the budget and authority to decide. Furthermore, when asking about their timeline for deciding, they would reply, "Can you get it here yesterday?"

Too bad we don't live in a perfect world.

Instead, it is more likely these days that we don't get right through to the decision maker—or to that mysterious "committee" that is going to decide at some undisclosed point in the future. There are usually some layers to go through first, before our product or service can finally get to the right set of eyes. Usually, the person standing in the way of the final decision maker is an influencer—someone who might weigh in on the decision but who doesn't have the final authority to make the ultimate decision.

Now here is the key: just because an influencer doesn't have the authority to make the final decision, that is not to say they don't know other crucial information that might help you navigate the decision tree and ultimately make a sale. Unfortunately, many sales reps are terrible at vetting or qualifying the influencer, so they just send their information and then hope for the best. If you follow the advice given here, you will not only know how to get this crucial information, but you will also separate yourself from 90 percent of the other sales reps who just don't know how to qualify influencers properly.

Questions to ask: even though your influencer might not be the final decision maker, they often have some insight into what the decision maker is looking for, or what their interest in your product or service is. Because this is true more times than it isn't, you must ask any of the following questions to get this insight. If the person you are talking to is hiding behind the real decision maker, ask any of the following questions.

Questions for Influencers

Qualifying the influencer—Question 1:

"_____, you probably work very closely with [the decision maker]. Tell me, how open are they to adding [your product or solution]?"

Qualifying the influencer—Question 2:

"_____, in terms of what you know, what is their [the decision maker or committee's] timeline for putting something like this into effect?"

Qualifying the influencer—Question 3:

"What other solutions are they considering right now?"

Qualifying the influencer—Question 4:

"How do you get involved in the decision on something like this?"

Qualifying the influencer—Question 5:

"How much influence (or input) do you have on the final decision?"

Qualifying the influencer—Question 6:

"How closely do you work with [the decision maker or committee]?"

(If they are involved):

"What are you recommending they do?"

Qualifying the influencer—Question 7:

"From what we have gone over so far, do you think this is something that would work for them?"

Qualifying the influencer—Question 8:

"Give me your thoughts on how [the decision maker] is going to decide who to pick for this"

Qualifying the influencer—Question 9:

"From what you know, what is [the decision maker] looking for in a solution like this?"

Qualifying the influencer—Question 10:

"Given what you know about the urgency for making this decision, how soon do you think they will decide on a solution?"

Qualifying the influencer—Question 11:

"In terms of budget, what are they thinking?"

Qualifying the influencer—Question 12:

"From your perspective, what is involved in their decision process?"

Qualifying the influencer—Question 13:

"How many other vendors are they going to look at before they make a decision?"

Qualifying the influencer—Question 14:

"From the other companies they are looking at, who are they leaning toward now?"

Qualifying the influencer—Question 15:

"Is the company they are using now still in the running?"

Layer:

"How likely do you think it is that they will just use the same company they are using now?"

Qualifying the influencer—Question 16:

"What do you think it will take for them to choose a different solution from who they are using now?"

Qualifying the influencer—Question 17:

"Is there any reason you can see that they would not move forward with something like this?"

Qualifying the influencer—Question 18:

"Is there anything you can think of that I should know that's important for them in making this decision?"

Qualifying the influencer—Question 19:

"What do you think I need to do to have the best shot of earning your business?"

As you can see, there are many areas and many questions you can ask that will give you tremendous insight into the sales process—if you just ask. Is the influencer going to know any or all of this? Of course not. But, again, more times than not, they will know a lot more than you might think. And if you begin asking some of these questions, you will know it, too!

THE ONLY QUALIFYING QUESTION YOU MAY NEED

I was working with a client the other day listening to one of their rep's qualifying call, and when the rep presented the cost of the product and asked if that fit within the prospect's budget, the prospect gave an interesting answer. She said:

"Well maybe, but it depends. I'll have to first see if what you have will work well enough for us to make the switch."

Question for you: What would you say next? In the call I was reviewing, the rep then said they should schedule a demo of the product and that during that demo the prospect would learn about how it worked and would then be able to decide. Is that what you would have done?

If you said yes, then you're wrong. Pitching this prospect without having a specific idea of what exactly they are looking for could prove to be a big waste of time. Think about it: Why would you want to spend an hour going over a demo wondering (or hoping) that what you said was enough to make them switch over to your company? This leads to the only qualifying question you may need.

The right thing to say here was: "And what specifically would you need to see to determine whether it would be worth switching or not?"

This question (and the other examples that follow) is the one question that will get your prospect to reveal what their precise buying motive is. Until you understand exactly what it is going to take to earn their business, you are "pitching blind." And this is how most sales reps operate. Many sales reps think the most important thing they can do is get prospects into their pipeline so they can demonstrate their product or service. They think that if they can do enough demos, then they will eventually make more sales.

Smart sales reps—the Top 20 Percent—think very differently. The Top 20 Percent want to know as much as possible in advance of the demo so they can tailor their presentation to the precise buying motives of each prospect. To do this, they are committed to asking the qualifying questions that will encourage a prospect to reveal what those buying motives are. The preceding question is specific to what this prospect said to the rep, but what follows are some other, more general questions that will achieve the same goal as well. Find ones that feel comfortable for you to use and then practice, drill, and rehearse until they become natural for you.

The Only Qualifying Question You May Need

Qualifying question 1:

"So_____, what specifically would you need to see in our demo next week that would convince you this would be a good fit for you?"

Qualifying question 2:

"And let me ask you this: What specifically would you like me to concentrate on during our presentation next week?"

Qualifying question 3:

"Tell me, _____, what area are you most interested in that I can address in detail during our presentation next week?"

Qualifying question 4:

"_____, what is the one thing that you are hoping this [your product or service] can do for you and your company?"

Qualifying question 5:

"And what would you need to see in the demo next week that would persuade you to move forward with this?"

Qualifying question 6:

"Just out of curiosity, what are three main things this (product or service) must do for you before you would decide to go with it?"

Qualifying question 7:

"_____, tell me, what one thing could you absolutely not live without? In other words, what must I be able to show you during the demo for you to be able to decide this could actually work for you?"

Qualifying question 8:

"What specifically are you hoping this will do for you?"

Qualifying question 9:

"_____, specifically, what is the one problem you are having that you hope this can fix for you?"

Qualifying question 10:

"And last, _____, what are you going to be looking to learn more about during our presentation next week?"

As you can see, once you uncover exactly what your prospect is looking for, then you will be able tailor your presentation to speak directly to that. I call this "speaking to your prospect's listening." Everybody is listening to what is most important to them, and knowing what this is in advance enables you to give the most effective presentation. The more you do this, the faster you will move into the Top 20 Percent of producers in your company.

HOW TO REQUALIFY EXISTING PROSPECTS AND CLIENTS

One area many sales reps struggle in is how to requalify existing accounts, or prospects they have not spoken with in a while. Let's first establish the need to do this, and then we will address exactly how to do it.

First, let us acknowledge that all things change. In fact, someone once said that the only thing that doesn't change is change itself. Change, in other words, is the only constant. That means that just because a prospect or client was in charge of a certain function last month or six months ago, it doesn't mean they are in charge of it today.

In addition to their duties changing, their areas of responsibilities change as well. Someone who was responsible for handling lead flow may now also be in charge of ordering those leads. And someone who was responsible for one area of the business (and ordering) may have given that responsibility to someone else. The bottom line is that when calling on existing accounts, it is important to do more than just, "Oh hi, just calling to see if you need anything?" Today, it is important that you requalify the person you are speaking with and try to find as many opportunities as possible to sell your product or service.

One of the biggest problems sales reps have is knowing how to transition into requalifying. The resistance I get from sales reps is, "But I spoke with him three months ago! I already know what he does (or what he needs, and so on)." "Yes," I answer. "But how many times have you found that things have changed since then?" If you are honest, the answer is that it changes all the time.

What you need to begin the requalifying process is a good transition sentence—a soft approach, so you can begin requalifying and get the updated information that often makes the difference between a successful call and one that results in nothing at all. Here are some examples of transition sentences. Feel free to adapt them to fit your personality and your product or service.

How to Requalify Existing Prospects and Clients

Transition sentence 1:

"_____, since it has been a few months since we have spoken, let me just make sure my information is correct. Besides yourself, who else handles...."

(This is an assumptive way to find out who the other decision makers in the company are.)

Transition sentence 2:

"_____, let me get up to date on things with you. I know that last time we spoke you said you handled training needs. What else are you responsible for these days?"

Transition sentence 3:

"Because things change all the time, let me just ask you a couple of quick questions to make sure I am up on things at your end. For example, what other products are you handling these days?"

Transition sentence 4:

"_____, I am updating the information on all of my accounts this month. Do you mind if I just verify a few things?"

(Wait for them to say yes.)

"Great! What is your current extension?"

And

"How about your direct phone number? Cell? Email?"

And

"And are you still the only contact for all the printing needs there now?"

And

"What other things are you handling now?"

And

"How about other departments? Who would I want to speak with. . . ."

And

"How about your need for [software, training, etc.]? Where have you been sourcing that these days?"

and

"What would you need to see from us to begin placing an order for that too?"

(I'm sure you can think of more. . . .)

Transition sentence 5:

"_____, I know the last time we spoke, you told me you handled [software, training, etc.]. Is that still correct?"

Layer

"Great. What else are you in charge of now?"

And

"How are you handling your [software, training, etc.]?"

And

"What other departments are handling the [software, training, etc.] now?"

And

"And what other products are you in charge of now?"

And

"And remind me again of the decision process there?"

And

"What is your timeline for this?"

And

"And besides yourself, who else would weigh in on this?"

As you can see, just because you think you know something about someone, you can still learn more. Think about it: When was the last time you were able to thoroughly qualify someone on the very first call? It probably took a few, didn't it? Each time you speak with an existing customer or account, you have the opportunity to learn more. This is how you uncover other opportunities and prospects. When you use these kinds of requalifying questions, you will be in a much better positon to completely qualify an opportunity, and that can only lead to more business.

THE TWO MOST IMPORTANT QUALIFIERS (AND HOW TO ASK FOR THEM)

If you had the chance to ask just only two qualifying questions, have you ever wondered what they might be? It is a good question because, as you know, prospects are often busy and many times you won't get the opportunity to ask everything you want to know. In the past, budget was the big stumbling block and the issue that sales reps really needed to drill down on. Don't think that budget isn't important today—it is. But now, with pricing being so transparent on websites and across social media, I don't think that budget qualifies anymore as one of the "Top Two" qualifiers.

Now remember the six main areas of qualifying that you need to cover are:

1. Why a prospect will buy (their buying motives)

2. Why a prospect might *not* buy (potential objections)

3. The budget parameters

4. Who the decision maker (or makers) is (are)

5. What their timeline is for making a decision

6. And who your competition is for this sale

For all you sales managers out there, if you want greater control over your team, and you want them to get out more qualified leads, then simply put a checklist together for each lead that goes into the pipeline, and make your reps get the answers for the six areas addressed here. And if you are a sales rep, remember you still must qualify for *all six* of these areas. Today, however, I have found that even more emphasis needs to be placed on the "Big Two" qualifiers given next. So if you have time for just two key areas, make sure you know about:

- Decision makers
- Competition

The reason these are now so important is because of the Internet. It is now estimated that because of the plethora of information available online (social media sites, websites, blogs, customer reviews, wholesale sites, and so forth) that over 60 percent of a sale is already determined before a prospect even talks to a sales rep. What this means is that the old sales standbys of yesterday—features and benefits—are far less important than they used to be, and that means competition and the decision tree are now more important.

So following are some techniques and questions you can use to qualify for these two important areas.

Qualifying Decision Makers

Qualifying the decision maker—Question 1:

"And _____, besides yourself, who else weighs in on this kind of a decision?"

Note: Asking this decision maker question in the assumptive ("who besides yourself") rather than the closed-ended way of ("Are you the decision maker....") often exposes who else is involved and can even reveal what the decision timeline is like, too.

Once they reveal they have to talk to their regional manager, boss, or partner, you can then begin drilling down on this. Use any of the following layering questions.

Layer:

"And how are you involved in the decision?"

Or

"And how much input do you have in this?"

Or

"And if you make a recommendation, do they usually go with it?"

Or

"Based on what you know of where they are leaning right now, do you think this is something they might be interested in?"

Or

"What do you know about their timeline for something like this?"

Or

"What is your gut telling you about the viability of this going through?"

Or

"What do you think they need to see to say yes on something like this?"

The point of layering your questions like this is so you can gather enough information to make your close easier later on. You see, nothing ambushes a closer more than getting to the end of a presentation only to be told that the prospect has to "show it to someone else." By qualifying in advance in this way, you will get information that you can then leverage at the end of your closing presentation to avoid falling into this trap.

Qualifying for Competition

Qualifying for competition—Question 1:

"And, _____, who else have you looked at for this?"

(If they tell you then layer with)

"And what do you think so far?"

Or

"And who do you like best so far?"

Then:

"And why is that?"

Or

"Who else are you going to reach out to for this?"

Then:

"And what are you hoping to accomplish by that?"

Or

"And why is it important to get several quotes?"

Qualifying the decision maker—Question 2:

"Who have you already looked at and said no to?"

Layer:

"And what about them wasn't a fit for you?"

Qualifying the decision maker—Question 3:

"Based on what you know of other company's offerings, what do you like best about us?"

Qualifying the decision maker—Question 4:

"If you had three very similar proposals on the table, what would be the deciding factor of who you would go with?"

Qualifying the decision maker—Question 5:

"What would you need to see from me to stop looking elsewhere?"

Asking these and other qualifying questions to uncover potential competitors will once again prevent you from being blindsided at the end of your presentation. Again, the Internet has changed the buying landscape for most companies and consumers, and it is crucial to know these (and the other four) areas well before you go into your closing presentation.

By using these questions, you will!

HOW TO QUALIFY PROSPECTS WITHOUT INTERROGATING THEM

While thinking about the two preceding qualifiers and looking at the various questions that are recommended, some of you may be wondering how you can ask these questions without sounding like you are interrogating your prospect. Admittedly, there is a fine line between having a dialogue with someone and asking enough questions to see whether they qualify for your product and service—but how exactly do you do that?

It is easy if you follow the next steps. Remember to always feel free to customize these questions to suit your personality and your product or service.

Step One: The first thing you need to do is frame an opening question that gives you the right to continue asking questions. Strange, I know, but the key word here is "frame" your question to earn the right to qualify. Here are some examples.

How to Earn the Right to Qualify

Earning the right to qualify—Question 1:

"_____, would it be okay if I asked you *just* a couple of quick questions to see if this would be a fit for you?"

Earning the right to qualify—Question 2:

"_____, it sounds like this might work for you. Do you mind if I ask you just a few questions so I can find the right fit?"

Earning the right to qualify—Question 3:

"_____, I know you are busy, and I'll be brief. There's just a few questions that will help give me an idea of what best to focus on when we next speak. Do you have just a couple of minutes for me now?"

Earning the right to qualify—Question 4:

"_____, let me get a clear idea of just a couple of areas of importance for you, and then I will be in the best situation to tailor a demo for you next week."

Earning the right to qualify—Question 5:

"_____, would you mind if I took a few minutes to ask you a couple of questions so I can understand exactly what you might need and how we can help?"

Framing your qualifying questions in this way always gives you some leeway with where to start and what to start asking. It also sets the right expectation for your prospect, and earns you a window to begin the qualification process.

Step Two: The way to seamlessly continue the qualification process is to use layering questions, when appropriate, to drill down on some of your prospect's answers. Layering questions are simply questions that tag on to the previous question, and they are used to get even more information on a specific area.

Most sales reps have never taken the time to learn the fine art of the layering question, and have not developed the ability to truly listen enough, which is a prerequisite for using them effectively. If you are willing to learn and use them, though, you will be rewarded with a wealth of information that will make the closing process that much easier. Here are some examples.

How to Use Layering Questions

Layering question examples—1:a

"And besides yourself, who else weighs in on the decision?"

Layer:

"And how do you figure into that?"

Or

"And how much influence do they have?"

Layering question examples—2:

"In terms of budget for this, how would our solution at [your price point] fit in right now?"

(If their budget is tight right now, or they are not sure, then use the following.)

"What other department or budget could you get the budget from if you really liked this?"

Or

"When you find something that you absolutely must have, where do you borrow the budget from?"

Or

"How have you made something like this fit in before?"

Layering question examples—3:

"What one thing can you think of that might prevent you from moving ahead on this in the next two weeks?"

Layer:

"And how would you get around that?"

Or

"How have you been able to sidestep that in the past?"

Or

"And what would you propose to do if that happens?"

As you can see, with the proper use of layering questions, you will not only learn more information about the important qualifying areas, but you will also be able to seamlessly continue the conversation. Layering questions allow you to extend the qualification phase naturally, as each question is a continuation of the question that was asked previously. This is the way you will earn the right to continue qualifying a prospect without sounding like you are interrogating him or her.

Step Three: Address any red flags that come up during the process. One of the biggest problems sales reps run into is hearing possible problem areas come up and then not addressing them. Many sales reps just hope these problems will go away or not come up again, but if they are honest, they know they never do go away. In fact, the truth about red flags is that they almost always come back up and often tend to ruin the deal in the end.

By addressing Red Flags when you learn about them, you not only have a chance to qualify them, but you also earn the right to keep asking questions while keeping your prospect engaged. Here are some examples.

How to Address Red Flags

Red flag example—1:

"Well, I'll have to run this by corporate."

Ask:

"What has their answer on something like this been in the past?"

Or

"And what do you think the chances of them approving this are?"

Or

"Based on where you see them leaning, what do you think they'll say?"

Then:

"How can we best get them to approve something like this?"

Red flag example—2:

"We are getting several quotes on this. . . ."

Ask:

"Which one do you like best so far?"

Or

"What does the winning quote have to look like, from your point of view?"

Or

"Our price point on this will be [software, training, etc.]. How do you think that will stack up with what you are willing to spend on something like this?"

Or

"And what do you think they will need to see to pick us?"

Red flag example—3:

"Well, we are in no hurry on this."

Ask:

"And what is your realistic time frame like?"

Or

"What might change that?"

Or

"What is going to motivate a decision to finally act on something like this?"

As you can see, asking questions of prospects—without sounding like you are interrogating them—is easy if you take the time in advance to prepare the right kinds of questions. Don't forget why you are asking all these qualifying questions: 80 percent of the sale is made during the qualification call! If you do this part of the process correctly, then your closing percentage will go up significantly. And if you don't thoroughly qualify, then you will likely just continue putting unqualified leads into your pipeline, and you already know how that turns out.

So reframe the prospecting call and learn how to earn the right to ask, and continue asking qualifying questions without sounding like you are interrogating your prospect. As you can see, it is easy if you know how.

CHAPTER 5

Other Prospecting Situations—and How to Handle Them

With all the new marketing opportunities companies have for generating leads—getting someone to "raise their hand" as they call it—prospects are becoming warmer and warmer. This has even led some sales experts to claim that, "Cold calling is dead!" Oh, if only the sales rep were so lucky. While the cold call may have become warmer, you still have to deal with relatively unknown prospects, even if they reach out and call in to you.

THE PROPER WAY TO HANDLE A CALL-IN LEAD

Because these prospects are still somewhat "cold"—meaning you don't have a relationship with them yet—even call-in leads can be tricky. Because reps often equate the implied interest of a call-in to being "qualified," they often skip some important steps. This can happen to all sales reps, and even happened to me recently.

A CEO called me the other day and wanted to know more about the kind of training I offered. Before I gave him my menu of services, I did what I teach and asked him how he found me, what motivated him to reach out to me, what he was looking for, and so on. I listened carefully as he revealed, in a candid way, what was happening with his inside sales team and what he was hoping to accomplish.

After he was done, I went over how I could help him and carefully matched up my customized solutions to each of the points he brought up. After a pause, he told me he would think about it and reach back out to me. Now, this is usually the time that I would qualify and close, but I was on vacation when this call took place, and I was more interested in getting back to the museum tour I was on than I was on closing the deal. (I know, shame on me.) But, when I was back in the office the following Monday, I reached out to this prospect and picked right up where I left off.

Here are two ways of handling a call-in lead. The first is what I should have done on the initial call, and the second is what I did on the next call the following Monday.

The Proper Way to Handle the First Call

After first hearing your prospect out and then matching up your product or services to them, you should then begin qualifying and even closing using the following questions and statements.

First call qualifying—Question 1:

"What is your timeline for getting this process started?"

(If they say, "As soon as possible")

"Okay—let me check my schedule [or your delivery/install schedule, and so on.] I see that I could have you on the calendar this coming Wednesday. Does that work for you?"

First call qualifying—Question 2:

"How does what I have described sound to you?"

(If they say, "Sounds good")

"Great—are you ready to put me to work for you today?"

First call qualifying—Question 3:

"Who else have you looked at for this so far?"

(If they say, "You are the first" or "A couple of people," then)

"How does our solution sound to you?"

(If they say, "Sounds good")

"Great—then let's look at our calendars and pick a date to get started...."

First call qualifying—Question 4:

"If this sounds good to you, are you in a position to get started today?"

(If they say, "I'll have to run this by [whomever]")

"I understand. Does what we have just gone over sound good to *you* so far?"

(If "yes")

"Okay then, let's go ahead and schedule a time to speak with [whomever they mentioned] and that way I will be able to answer their questions as well...."

Do you see how I am moving the call to either a close or setting up the next step? At each phase, I am taking their pulse and directing and keeping control of the call.

Asking Questions on the Second Call

Second call qualifying—Question 1:

"Hi, this is _____ and I just wanted to get back with you regarding our last call. Now I know you were interested in (your service or product), and I don't know how many other companies you have spoken with or where you are in the process?"

[Now hit mute and listen.]

Second call qualifying—Question 2:

"Hi, this is _____ and I wanted to get back with you regarding our last call. Now I know you were interested in (your service or product), and I wanted to know what your timeline for getting started with this is...."

(Now hit mute and listen.)

Second call qualifying—Question 3:

"Hi, this is _____ and I wanted to get back with you regarding our last call. Now I know you were interested in [your service or product], and I wanted to know what other questions you might have?"

(Now hit mute and listen.)

Based on what their answers are to the preceding questions, you can pick up where you left off the last time and resume asking the questions from the first preceding script (direct the prospect toward the close). Either way, just remember that when you receive a call-in lead, you need to still qualify and close. And if you forget or get rushed off the phone, the key is to call back within a day or two to resume qualifying. When you do, take the call as far as you can using the scripts just listed.

FEATURES AND BENEFITS VERSUS KNOWING HOW TO SELL

I had a landscaper install a new sprinkler system the other day, and as we stood under the warming sun waiting for his crew to set up, he asked me what I did for a living. I told him I was a sales trainer (this is the easiest answer, as for some reason when I add "inside sales," people outside of the industry have no idea what I'm talking about).

He immediately made the mistake that most companies, managers, and even sales reps make when he said next, "Product knowledge is what it's all about. You have to know your products."

When I corrected him by saying product knowledge takes second place to qualifying a prospect and discovering unique buying motives, he seemed genuinely confused. I explained: "Most companies spend hours, weeks, and even months training their sales reps on each product and service, and then about a day (or a couple of hours) on how to sell them. This results in a knowledgeable sales team that is quick to list features and benefits until the prospect yawns and says he has to go. This creates a lot of conversations, but not a lot of sales."

"What should they be doing?" he asked.

And that is when I asked him how he would go about selling me a pencil. He thought about it for a while and then launched into—you bet—a list of features and benefits of a pencil. I let him go on for a while until he was out of ideas (you can only talk about the color yellow and the use of an eraser for so long), and then I asked him: "What if I don't even use pencils?"

That stumped him.

And that is the whole point. Most sales reps sell just like he does: leading with features and benefits sure that if they just say the right one or enough of them, in the right order or combination, then prospects will eventually see some value and say, "Ah! I've got to have that! Thank you so much for calling!"

If this is what you or your sales team does, then I'd repeat Dr. Phil's question, "How's that working out for you?"

The proper way to sell a pencil—and your product or service—is to first qualify for need and unique buying motives, timeline, buying history, decision makers and process, and so forth, and then match up the appropriate features and benefits to fit those defined needs.

So using the "how to sell a pencil" analogy, it doesn't begin by pitching the attributes of a No. 2 pencil. Rather, it starts by uncovering the need for one (or a shipment of a thousand). It begins with a series of questions like:

"How do you use pencils in your facilities?"

"How many pencils do you go through in a month? A year?"

"Who orders the pencils?"

"What's important to you in a pencil?"

"How many pencils do you usually order at a time?"

"Where do you get your pencils from now?"

"Why do you get them there?"

"When was the last time you compared suppliers of pencils?"

"If you were to change suppliers, what would be important for you in the next vendor?"

"Besides yourself, who makes the decision to order pencils?"

"How about in your other facilities? Who orders for them?"

And so on. Now, I can just hear some of you thinking, "But Mike, a prospect isn't going to sit still for all these questions!" Well, maybe yes, maybe no. I can tell you now, non-buyers won't sit still, but most buyers will answer some, if not all of those questions. And that is a clue as to who might buy from you and who won't. Also, while buyers may not have the time to answer all of your questions, you can at least prioritize your questions so you ask the most important ones up front. You can requalify later, as you will see.

The bottom line is that you can't sell without knowing if there is a need and an interest. And if you ask some of the answers offered here, then you'll know exactly how to pitch and how to sell. If you don't, you will just go through your list of features and benefits and when you get to the end, you will cross your fingers and hope someone buys.

I don't know about you—but that is a horrible way to make your way through life in sales.

HOW TO BUILD INSTANT RAPPORT WITH C-LEVEL EXECUTIVES

I was recently asked by a client to make some cold calls into an upper C-level suite, to set appointments for his outside sales team to show the inside team how it is done. His inside team first had trouble getting these busy people on the phone, and then getting past the first paragraph of their script before getting brushed off.

I had listened to their calls and immediately recognized the problem: the reps were not taking the time to immediately assess the prospect's mood and connect with them. They were instead coming off like sales reps, and the executives who they did reach weren't having any of that.

If you call into the upper C suites, here is what I did (and you should be doing) to connect with and give yourself a chance to have a conversation with them.

1. Before you leave a voice mail, try calling three to five times to reach them first.

Vary the times of your calls, on the same day and on different days, to see if you can reach them.

I have done this for many years, and it is amazing how many people you will get on the phone if you just persevere.

2. When you do get them on the phone, immediately assess their style of communication by how they answer the phone. Are they in a hurry? Are they a driver? Or, are they laid back, relaxed and at lunch?

It is crucial that you match their pacing and their energy in these initial seconds of the call or else you will just come off as a sales rep who is going to waste their time. For example, when one COO answered the phone, he was short and somewhat demanding. I immediately said: "John, thanks for picking up the phone, I'll make this brief...." Then I went into a two-sentence value statement and asked him a question. He appreciated that I didn't begin reading a sales pitch at him, and he gave me a considered answer to my question.

3. Matching a prospect's style or mood is important. If you find someone who seems somewhat laid back or at least not in a hurry to bite your head off, then connect with that person by talking about something else—briefly—before you pitch them.

For example, I called into a company, and the hold music was the rock song, "Sweet Home Alabama." When the prospect picked up the phone, I immediately complimented him on the hold music and asked him if that was his personal choice. He said it came with the phone system, and we talked about the song briefly. Only after that did I tell him who I was and begin my pitch.

This technique also works well with subjects like the weather ("Is it hailing there, too?"), and the day of the week "I hope Monday is treating you okay" or "I don't know about you, but I'm happy it's almost Friday...."

By the way, it is always best to lead off with these kinds of rapport-building techniques *before* you announce your name and company name. If you announce first, then you have put the "salesman" target on your forehead, and it is too late. The key is that you must have the right personality to do this. If you try this with a driver, your call will end right there.

1. Be absolutely prepared to overcome the "I wouldn't be interested" blow-off. You must have an effective comeback to that blow-off memorized and be ready to automatically deliver it. This is especially true for when you get a C-level executive on the phone, because when you do, you have about a nanosecond to make a connection.

My rebuttal to "I'm not interested" is something along the lines of:

> "That's fine and I'm not trying to sell you something today. Instead, I think I have an alternative solution for your [software needs, training, etc.] and just want to find the best way to show it to you. Believe me, you'll be happy you learned about it...."

You can also use any of the previously scripted-out best-practice techniques in the previous section.

2. "Briefly" is a word that gives you the best shot of being able to give your next couple of sentences. Try: "_____, thanks for taking the call. Briefly, what I'm calling you about is...." Then make it *brief*. Get to a question quickly to either engage your prospect or give him or her the chance to tell you he or she is still not interested or that he or she is not the right person, and so on.

The point is to engage your prospect—not talk at them.

3. Let your prospect talk! After you have delivered your two sentences (better make them good!), it is time to let your C-level executive talk. *Don't* interrupt. Hit your mute button. These people are used to talking and to having people listen to them. If you do that, you will gain their respect, and they will give you a chance to speak when it's your turn (usually).

The point of all these tips is that you have to connect with your C-level exec and meet them on their level. You can't just go into your pitch at your own speed and expect them to politely listen and follow you. They won't. Also, you have much less time with this kind of prospect, so it is crucial that you get to the point—and to a question—quickly.

By following these techniques, you will separate yourself from all your competition that is calling and delivering a monologue on their product or service. By learning and using the techniques and scripts discussed here, you will have the best chance of actually connecting with them and having a chance to get your value statement across.

CHAPTER 6

Voice Mail and Email Strategies

Even though voice mail and email are so prevalent—even to the point of being abused—they are still a very effective prospecting tool—if used correctly. Unfortunately, this part of a sales rep's arsenal is underdeveloped, and very few sales professionals are being taught the proper way to use these techniques. There are, however, a set of best practices that you will learn in this chapter that will separate you from your competition, and that will get your prospects to take notice of you. Many prospects will even reach back out to you, and the others will be much more receptive to you once you do reach them by phone.

You will find here two strategies that will help you immensely. The first is how to develop and leave an effective voice mail message—complete with what to do and what not to do. The next is how to combine voice mail with an email campaign to reach maximum effectiveness.

Study, adapt, and then use the following techniques, and you will soon have plenty of prospects to speak with and to qualify for your product or service.

VOICE MAIL: FIVE PROVEN TECHNIQUES THAT GET YOUR CALLS RETURNED

If you are struggling to get your voice mail messages returned, then you are not alone.

Industry statistics show that less than 10 percent of voice mails to new prospects are returned. Because of this, finding the right voice mail message and knowing a few proven techniques, can be the key to not only contacting those hard-to-reach sales leads, but also to developing relationships and getting new accounts.

Here are five proven techniques that give you the best chance of getting your voice mail messages returned.

Proven Technique Number One:

Don't even leave a voice message! Sounds strange, doesn't it? The truth is that the best technique to follow when trying to reach a prospect for the first time is to persevere and call five or seven times first before leaving a message. Your goal is to catch your prospect picking up the phone and then have a conversation with him or her rather than leaving multiple unreturned voice mails.

Try calling at different times of the day, and even several times on Friday. Fridays are the most relaxed days, and most people are getting ready for the weekend instead of gearing up for the week. The worst day to leave a voice mail? Monday.

One caveat: for those of you who are worried that when you do finally catch someone who picks up the phone and is upset that you didn't leave a message (yet they saw that you called several times), be prepared with a good script. Something like: "I didn't want to bother you with several voice mail messages, so I decided to just try to catch you live instead. I hope that didn't inconvenience you. Anyway, I am glad we are finally speaking...."

Persevering in this way is *the best* way to actually get someone on the phone, and because most sales reps won't do it, you are going to be way ahead if you do.

Proven Technique Number Two:

You must script out an effective voice mail message in advance. Nothing will get your message deleted faster than the sound of an unprepared and unprofessional message filled with um's and ah's.

As soon as a busy prospect hears that kind of message, especially from someone they do not know (and from a salesperson on top of that!), they automatically reach for the delete button. Don't you?

You should also make sure your scripted voice mail has these three elements:

1. Put the focus on your prospect—*not* on your product or service.

2. Don't ever say, "I'd like to take some time to learn more about you...."

3. Make sure to leave your number *slowly*, and two times.

As you will see in the following examples, most sales reps leave a message that is all about them—and this never works. Second, sometimes they think that by wanting to "learn more about how you handle...." they think that they are putting the prospect first. *Wrong.* All the prospect is thinking is that they don't want to take their valuable time to educate you so you can sell them something.

And three, the worst technique of all is leaving your phone number so quickly that you force your prospect to replay your message over and over again just to get your phone number. (Like anybody is going to do that.)

Proven Technique Number Three:

Turn a bad VM message into an effective one.

The wrong way to leave a VM (and unfortunately, how most people do it):

> "Hi, this is [your name] with [your company], and we offer shipping supplies and packaging for all your shipping needs. The reason I am calling is to learn a little more about your business and to find out more about your shipping needs and see if we can save you some money. If you would call me back at 888-555-1234 that would be great. Look forward to hearing from you soon."

This message checks all the "do not do" boxes I have listed in Technique Number Two. It is all about the caller. It wants to take time from the prospect so they can pitch more, and the number was only left once (and usually too fast for the prospect to copy it down).

Here Is the Right VM to Leave

"Hi, [prospect's name] this is [your name] with [your company]. We offer discounted shipping supplies and packaging, and if you're like most companies we work with, then you're probably paying too much! Our clients save between 10 and 15 percent each month and get better service, guaranteed. To find out how much you can save, just give me a call at (*slowly* leave your phone number.)

"Once again, my name is [your name], and my toll-free number is: [leave number slowly again]. If I don't hear back from you in the next couple of days, I'll reach out to you again. If you'd prefer to be taken off our list, or if you'd prefer to get some information by email, just give me a ring and leave me a message. Talk to you soon!"

This VM is effective because it is focused on the prospect and what is in it for them (10 to 15 percent savings). The phone number was left two times *slowly*, but the magic technique was that *you gave your prospect a way out!* You let them know that they can simply call you back, leave you a message (so they won't have to speak with you or be pitched when they call), and they can remove themselves from being called by you again if they aren't interested. This is good for you, too, as you won't waste your time with uninterested prospects.

One note: if you find the preceding message too long, edit it. Script your VM the way you like it, and then use it consistently. In fact, spend some time now reworking your existing voice mail message so that it conforms to the rules just described.

Proven Technique Number Four:

Combine your voice mails with an email campaign for maximum effectiveness. The number one law in all marketing is repetition. That's why Coca-Cola still buys millions of dollars of ads every year.

It's the same with getting your prospects to notice you. The most effective way is by using a two-month-long campaign that goes like this:

First: Try to reach someone for a couple of days without leaving a VM.

Week One: Leave one VM and follow it up with an email that same day. Then leave a second VM that same week.

Week Two: Send email number 2, then leave a VM at the beginning of the week and on that Friday.

Week Three: Send an email at the beginning of the week and at the end. Leave a VM in between.

Week Four: Send another email on Tuesday, and leave a VM on that Thursday.

Month Two: Send *either* one email or leave one VM per week for four weeks. (Also: Call in between and don't leave a message.)

Any time between weeks three and four, one of your emails needs to be the "Should I Stay or Should I Go" email. If you have not heard of this email, then your return contact rate is about to go up by 60 percent! It goes like this:

Subject line: [prospect's first name] Should I Stay or Should I Go?

Body of Email:

Dear _____:

I haven't heard back from you, and that tells me one of three things:

You don't have a need at this time or you have already chosen another company for this.

You might be interested but haven't had the time to get back to me yet.

You've fallen and can't get up. In that case, please let me know, and I'll call 911 for you....

Please let me know which one it is because I'm starting to worry!

Honestly, all kidding aside, I understand you are really busy, and the last thing I want to do is be pain in the neck once a week. Whether your schedule has just been too demanding or you've gone in another direction, I would appreciate it if you would take a second to let me know so I can follow up accordingly. Thank you in advance and I look forward to hearing back from you.

Kind Regards,

If you are smiling while reading this, so will your prospect. Again, this is a high percentage email that gets a response about 60 percent of the time. Compare that to your current results.

Proven Technique Number Five: If your VM and email campaigns don't work, then consider going that extra mile. (As a top producer once said, "The extra mile is never crowded.") Even though a prospect may not be in the market now, we all know that things change. When they do, you want to be top of mind so they are thinking about you when they finally are ready to make a purchase.

The most effective way to do this is by sending actual greeting cards. The easiest way to do that is by using a company I use called Send Out Cards. (You can learn more about them here: www.sendoutcards .com/mrinsidesales).

I have been using SOC for years and they have made me a lot of money (hundreds of thousands of dollars, in fact) in sales to prospects I would not have gotten if I hadn't been drip marketing to them regularly. I use SOC for many reasons, including:

- It's extremely affordable to send a high-quality card with a real stamp.

- It's easy and fast—you create the cards in advance and they send them automatically without you having to do anything more!

- You can build "campaigns" so you can send cards at any interval you choose (and you can build lots of campaigns).

- Every card is completely customizable—you can choose from 15,000-plus of their beautiful cards (and include your own message) or you can completely create your own with your own images.

It is highly effective. In fact, did you know that the number one salesperson in the world—according to the *Guinness Book of World Records*—is a guy named Joe Girard? He was a car salesman, and he sold an average of six new cars *every day!* How did he do it? He sent a card to every customer and every prospect every month (and one for Christmas)—13 cards in all. Joe was so successful that people had to make appointments with him to buy a car!

The good news is that sending physical greeting cards will work in your business as well.

And www.sendoutcards.com/mrinsidesales can make it easy and effective for you.

So there you have it: the five proven voice mail techniques to get your calls returned.

Follow them and you will be much more successful than you are now. Don't follow them and, well, you already know how that goes.

THE TOUCH-POINT PLAN: HOW TO TURN COLD LEADS INTO WARM LEADS

Staring at a list of cold names you have to call can be discouraging. Calling those names and leaving voice mails that never get returned is even more discouraging. And finally reaching someone only to be quickly blown off can be downright heartbreaking! Don't you wish there was a way to turn cold names into warm leads?

There is!

It is called a "touch-point plan," and it is very effective if you do it right. A touch-point plan is simply a combination of carefully scripted voice messages and emails used in combination over a period of time. How many messages and over what period of time is variable, and I have seen many studies recommend roughly six phone calls and five emails over a month's time.

I have been successfully using a bit less—five to seven total messages—but I supplement this strategy by making calls in between trying to catch the prospect picking up their phone. If they don't answer, I don't leave a voice mail. Sometimes I opt for a longer campaign—up to two months as mentioned in the earlier section on voice mail.

What type of a touch-point plan you decide to develop (how many calls and emails) can depend on many factors such as whether it is a business-to-business call—and what your target prospect's title is—or whether it is a business-to-consumer call and what hours you are calling. You will find what your sweet spot is if you just experiment a bit.

The bottom line, though, is that the more times you reach out to a prospect, the more likely it is they will become familiar with you and your company. Many prospects will respect your professional and persistent attempts to reach them. Because of this, when you finally do reach a prospect, you will have built some recognition and credibility, and your prospect will be more willing to give you a bit of their time.

This is how you turn a cold lead into a warm lead.

I have listed in this section a sample touch-point plan that involves two voice messages and three emails. I first make about a week of calls without leaving a voice mail (assuming I don't reach the prospect), and then I spread the following touch-point plan over two weeks.

If I have not gotten a response or reached anyone after the touch-point plan, I wait a week, and then spend the fourth week calling again without leaving a message. I have had *a lot* of success with this plan and at the end of the four-week period, I have generally reached those prospects who are reachable.

Here is a sample touch-point plan, with generic wording, that you can customize to fit your company and product or service.

Voice Mail 1

"Hi _____, this is [your full name] with [your company].

"_____, I'm calling about [your brief value prop—example: "the effectiveness of your online marketing"].

"I wanted to briefly introduce you to a way to save as much as 25 percent over what you may be spending now, and still maintain or even increase the effectiveness of your results.

"If you would give me a quick call back at: [your number] we can set a time to speak.

"Once again, my name is [your full name], with [your company name] and my number is [your number, slowly].

"I'll follow this up with an email and another call to you if I don't hear back. Have a good afternoon."

Email 1 (to Be Sent Right after You Leave Your First Voice Mail)

Subject Line: [first name], I just left you a voice mail

Body of email:

[first name],

This is [your full name] with [your company]. Sorry I missed you.

I understand that you are in charge of your online marketing, and I wanted to set up a time to briefly speak with you later this week. (If you are not in charge of the advertising, please forward this to the person who is).

We have a new way of maximizing your online advertising spend that reduces what your current spend is, yet it also reaches more of the customers that fit your ideal demographic. [Obviously, insert your value prop here.] Our model is so effective that you can literally save up to 25 percent over what you're spending now!

I'd like to schedule a brief conversation to explain how this would work with your company, and I guarantee you will at least come away with a whole new way of looking at your online marketing.

If you would reach back out to me with a couple of days and times that might work, that would be great.

If I don't hear back, I will reach out to you again next week. Looking forward to connecting with you.

[your name and company signature]

Voice Mail 2: (Three to Four Days Later)

"Hi, _____, this is [your full name] once again with [your company]. My number is [leave your number, slowly].

"_____, you probably received a voice mail from me already, and I also sent you an email along with a brief description of how we save companies up to 25 percent on their online advertising, while in many cases increasing their results. [your value prop.]

"I'd like to spend a few minutes on the phone with you next week, and I guarantee that it will be worth your time.

"If you would give me a quick call back to let me kno a day and time that would work for you, that would be appreciated. My direct phone number again is: [your phone number].

"I'll follow up again with you if I don't hear back. Have a great day."

Email 2: (Send This Email One to Two Days after Your Second Voice Mail)

(Include an online brochure of your company and services)

Subject Line: [first name], second attempt to reach you

Body of Email:

[first name],

This is [your full name] with [your company name] once again.

I hope you have received my messages, and today I wanted to include some information on our company and a brief description of what we do.

As I mentioned earlier, we help companies reduce what they spend on their online advertising by as much as 25 percent while maintaining or even increasing their results. [your value prop]

I'm sure that when you compare what we do to what you're doing now, you will want to know more.

I would simply like a few minutes to see if what we do would be a good fit for you. Once we speak, I guarantee you'll come away with some good ideas, regardless of what you're doing now.

I will give you a call in a few days, after you've digested the attached information. Or, you can reach back out to me to let me know your interest level.

(your name and company signature)

Voice Mail 3: (Final VM—Leave Three to Four Days after the Second Email)

Hi _____, this is [your full name] with [your company] again.

I'm sorry we haven't been able to connect yet. As you may know, we offer a unique way of increasing the effectiveness of your online marketing while reducing what you are currently spending by as much as 25 percent. [your value prop]

You may be involved in another initiative right now, so I don't want to bother you if you are busy or if you are not interested.

When you get this message, could you either call back and leave me a voice mail or just respond to one of the emails I've sent you?

Just let me know what the next appropriate step would be for us to connect.

You can reach me by calling [your number, slowly], or you can email me at: [your email address]

I really appreciate you taking the time to get back with me.

Thanks, and have a great day.

Once you have customized and tested the voice mails and emails in this touch-point plan, you will know whether you need to add another one or two messages. Just test a variation of plans and see what the best results are for you. Don't forget to add in calls the week before and after the plan as well!

The most important part of a successful touch-point plan is to consistently use one. Most sales reps fail to reach back out to prospects (both inbound and outbound leads), and many just make one attempt and then move on. The way to double or even triple your sales and income is to be detail-oriented and to persevere until you reach your prospects.

Adopting the approach described here will separate you from 90 percent of the other sales reps in your industry and this will increase your effectiveness exponentially.

CONCLUSION TO PROSPECTING TECHNIQUES AND SCRIPTS

As stated earlier, the cold or prospecting call is the most important part of the sales cycle.

This is where you identify real buyers, and where you learn what it will take to close your prospect. By learning and following the strategies and word-for-word scripts in this section, you will have an advantage over your competition and can quickly improve both the quality of your prospects and your closing ratios and results. This means more money for you and your family.

But did you notice I said, "learning" and not reading? It is not enough for you to just read the scripts and techniques in this section. You need to study them, adapt them, and then make it a habit to use them over and over again. This is what Dale Carnegie[*], in his

---

[*]The reference from the book "How to Win Friends and Influence People" is mentioned in the respective p. xxii.

best-selling book, *How to Win Friends and Influence People*, said when he quoted George Bernard Shaw. "Shaw once remarked: 'If you teach a man anything, he will never learn.' Shaw was right. Learning is an active process. We learn by doing. So, if you desire to master the principles you are studying in this book, do something about them. Apply these rules at every opportunity. If you don't, you will forget them quickly. Only knowledge that is used sticks in your mind."

I couldn't have said it better about the techniques, strategies, and scripts in *this* book. Only by putting these techniques to work for you will you be able to overcome the old ideas and habits you are currently using to get unsatisfactory results. Doing so will take a commitment of both time and energy, but the investment you make now will pay dividends to you for the rest of your career. I can tell you from personal experience that once you elevate your skill set and begin seeing better results, you never go back. Once you become a Top 20 Percent producer, you remain that way—no matter what product or service you end up selling.

PART III

CLOSING TECHNIQUES AND SCRIPTS

CHAPTER 7

How to Close the Sale

With a renewed emphasis on qualifying prospects more thoroughly during the prospecting phase, you should now have much better leads in your pipeline to give presentations to. And because the quality of your prospects is better, you can now approach the close—or presentation or demo stage—much differently as well. The old way of closing, the "spray and pray" method in which you just pitch and pitch *at* the prospect and then ask for the sale at the end, hoping and praying they say yes, should be abandoned completely for a more engaging and consultative approach.

Your goal now is to check in with your prospect throughout the sale, slowly build a yes momentum, and get buy-in throughout the selling process. By adopting this more collaborative approach, asking for the sale at the end becomes a natural result of the closing process, and one where the prospect is saying yes much more often.

In this chapter, I'll give you some solid tools and techniques to help you engage your prospect and create a more balanced, two-way conversation. Included in this section are ways to get your prospect engaged, ways of requalifying a prospect if you didn't learn everything on the first call, and also ways of handling initial resistance you sometimes get when a prospect either doesn't have the time for your presentation or has changed their mind for another reason. You will also learn how and when to begin handling objections during this opening phase of your presentation, as well as some strategies to be more effective with your time. Overall, this section will help you feel more prepared and confident going into your closing call.

In chapter eight, "How to deal with specific objections," you will find a fresh approach to handling some of the recurring objections you get the majority of the time. "I haven't looked at the information yet," and the persistent objection, "I need to think about it," along with many other common objections are addressed in this section. You will find multiple word-for-word examples on how to handle each of these objections, and I encourage you to use the ones that resonate with you. You will also learn how to deal effectively with the influencer as well as how to handle other stalls such as when your prospect wants to check references or claims that they are doing business with a relative or friend. You will find current and effective ways to deal with and overcome these and many other objections and closing situations you may be struggling with now.

Then, in chapter nine, "Winning closing techniques," you will find even more word-for-word scripts and strategies to help you build momentum during your presentation and handle other situations you run across during your selling presentations. What might be the most important piece of advice here is asking for the sale five times or more—at least! Over the years, I've found that the true art of closing—whereby you listen to an objection, isolate the true problem, address it, and then ask for the sale again—has been lost. Today, most sales reps give up much too easily at the first sign of resistance or an objection. Learning how to persevere and win the sale is an advanced technique that takes patience, confidence, and lots of proven techniques and strategies. If done professionally, and in the right situations, this ability to build value and convey an urgent sense of belief in your product or service can and does often make the difference in whether your prospect buys from you or your competition.

Finally, in chapter ten, I will address what to do if the sale doesn't close right away. The best way to schedule a call back and follow up with prospects is laid out word-for-word, and I give a final shout-out to the power of sending cards. Whether you choose to handwrite a card or use a company to do it automatically for you, what I have found over the years is that if a prospect has a need for my product or service, that need rarely goes away. Things change all the time, and when they change once again for my prospect, I want to be sure that I am top of mind so that their next phone call is an easy choice—me! Developing an automatic card campaign that sends a personalized and customized card to my prospects over the course of 12 months has proven to be the most effective way I have found of doing just that.

You will learn many proven and valuable techniques in this third section on closing, and once again I encourage you not to just read this material but rather to study it, break it down, and adapt the scripts and techniques to fit your personality and your product or service. Once you do, then practice, drill, and rehearse these techniques and scripts, and record and analyze yourself so you can improve on every phone call. If you make this commitment to yourself, I guarantee that your closing results will go up dramatically. You will begin making more sales and seeing more money each week in your paycheck, but perhaps even more importantly, you will begin feeling much more confident when you are on the phone working with a prospect. That is when sales finally becomes fun, and even easy. In truth, that is how sales should be: helping someone who has a real need and desire to buy the best solution to help them—yours.

OPENING A CLOSING CALL

How do you open your closing presentation calls? Have you scripted out the best opening, or do you wing it? Do you let your prospect take the lead, by asking if this is still a good time for them, or do you confidently and enthusiastically assume the opening and set the pace for the rest of the call? The way you open your closing call often determines how the presentation will go, and many sales reps set themselves up for stalls by opening a closing call weakly. Here are some wrong ways to open your closing calls.

Wrong Opening Call

The Wrong Opening—1:

> "Oh hi, this is _____ with _____, and we had an appointment right now to go over the presentation. Is this still a good time for you?"

Now I know that it seems polite to check in with your prospect before just launching into your presentation, but giving them an out right at the beginning isn't the way to go. When you use the opening I recommend here, if the time isn't right for your prospect, they will let you know, but don't open your call like the preceding example by giving them an out.

The Wrong Opening—2:

"Oh hi, this is _____ with _____, and I was just checking in with you to see if you needed anything today?"

Although this may immediately sound weak to you (and it is), you would be shocked by how many calls I listen to that sound just this way! This kind of opening might as well be restated as, "Ah, you wouldn't want to buy anything today, would you?" Once again, the cure is to script out an assumptive opening that offers them a choice of products or specials, as you will read later.

The Wrong Opening—3:

"Hi, this is _____ with _____. How are you today?"

Nothing screams a sales call more than those four overused words: "How are you today?"

Be different! Be engaging! Use an opening that separates you from your competition and that what they are going to experience with you is more than just a worn-out sales pitch.

Now that we have some examples of what *not* to do, let us look at some alternative ways of opening your closing call.

Right Opening Call

The Right Opening—1:

"Hi, _____, this is _____ with _____. How's your Friday going?"

(Listen and react accordingly.)

"_____, I've been looking forward to speaking with you today because I have some updates that you will be particularly interested in. I'm sure you're in front of a computer, so do me a favor and go to. . . ."

Once again, if this is not a good time for your prospect (but it should be because you did send out reminder emails, right?), then they will tell you. The power of this opening is that you are opening with some exciting news. You are directing them into the presentation, and you are taking control of the call. And that is what you should always be doing.

The Right Opening 2:

"Hi, _____, this is _____ with _____. I hope you're having a good day so far."

"Great! _____, I'm glad I reached you, and after you hear about some of the specials we have going on today, you'll be glad I called. Now the last time we spoke you told me you were [heavy users of/always on the lookout for/usually in need of....], and the good news is that today we have insert offer and price and they are flying out the door. How many of these could I ship out to you today?"

Assumptive, assumptive, assumptive. This opening is great for a commodities type of sale such as pharmaceuticals, disposables, or other supplies. Now, are they always going to buy? Of course not! But when you assume the sale and lead-in with a couple of specials that you know they could be interested in, and then when you ask for an order like that, those prospects who might be interested in what you have will likely take the bait and either order or begin asking you buying questions. And that is what you are looking for, right?

The Right Opening 3:

"Hi, _____, this is _____ with _____. Is it still raining out there?"

Again, throw away the old, tired opening of "How are you today?" and replace it with a different and engaging opening that anchors your prospect into the day and actually gets them thinking about how their day actually is going. I have already added different examples to the preceding two openings, and you can see how much better they flow. By using any one of these, you will be building a lot more rapport by asking this, and I encourage you to try it and see for yourself how effective it is.

When you combine these openings with the requalifying scripts you will read further on, you will have the most effective and comprehensive opening possible. It is this type of opening that will give you the edge over your competition and get you further into a qualified presentation, and that will result in more closed sales.

FIVE WAYS TO GET BETTER AT HANDLING OBJECTIONS

I coach a lot of sales professionals, one on one, in individual sessions every week. Sales managers, business owners, and individual sales reps who are committed to moving into the Top 20 Percent or Top 5 Percent of their profession choose the individual attention they get. Before working with someone, I send out a "coaching intake" form that they fill out and return to me before our first session. This gives me insight into their situation and particular sale, what they want to work on, what is standing in their way, and what they hope to accomplish during our time together.

When working with individual sales reps, one of the most common requests I get is that they would like to get better at handling objections. I tell them all the same thing: "if you just do exactly as I will teach you to do, then in 60 days, you will know exactly how to handle objections, and you will no longer be scared when your prospect or client brings one up."

In fact, I tell them, you will even welcome them!

So what's the secret? Well, there are five of them, really, and I list them in this section. If you want to get better at handling objections, if you want to confidently learn to handle or overcome them like the top pros, then simply follow the secrets I give you here.

Secret Number One:

Take time to carefully script out rebuttals to the common objections you get day in and day out (have you taken the time to do this yet?). Remember, the best thing about sales is that you get the same objections, stalls, and put-offs over and over again. You already know what's coming!

The true pros recognize this and take the time to script out best-practice responses to them so that when they get them, they can confidently and effectively handle them.

Other sales reps still choose to ad-lib their responses, which means they are making up one poor response after another. This is why they are discouraged and unsuccessful. So take some time right now and script out your best-practice responses so you will never have to scramble for what to say again!

Secret Number Two:

Memorize your best-practice responses. Remember what Don Shula of the Miami Dolphins said: "Overlearning means that the players are so prepared for a game that they have the skill and confidence needed to make the big play." P. 74, "Everyone's a Coach," by Ken Blanchard & Don Shula (Zondervan, HarperCollinsPublishers)

Again, it is the same in sales. By internalizing your best-practice responses to objections, you will be able to handle them automatically, without thinking or stressing.

Secret Number Three:

To effectively memorize your rebuttals, you will need to put in some time. The most effective way to memorize and internalize your rebuttals is to record them into a recording device (and you are already carrying one of these around in your pocket—all smartphones have one), and then commit to listening to them 30 to 50 times.

This is the same thing you did to learn the words to your favorite song, and it works for rebuttals to objections as well. In fact, you will even remember the exact inflection and pacing as well, so make your recording sound just as you'd like to deliver the rebuttal in a sales situation.

Secret Number Four:

Record your actual sales calls and listen to how you sound when delivering your rebuttals. Listen for if you are using the right rebuttal to the objection your prospect or client just gave you.

By recording yourself, you will learn tons of things that will make you better, including how to deliver your rebuttals more convincingly. You will also learn whether or not your rebuttal is the best one to use, which leads me to secret number five.

Secret Number Five:

Be prepared to revise your rebuttals when you need to. After listening to your sales calls over and over again, you will keep finding ways to improve. Perhaps a rebuttal can be shortened? Maybe it can include a few key words or phrases. Perhaps you could deliver it with a bit more energy. Or less energy.

Never stop learning, critiquing, and getting better. The top professionals in any industry are always adapting, always learning, and always improving. You should, too.

So there you have it: the five ways to get better at handling objections. If these sound familiar to you—and if I am beginning to sound like a broken record—it is because these are the fundamental things you can do to improve. If you are thinking that you have heard these before, my question to you is, "Yes, but when was the last time you did any of them?" Or better, "Are you doing them all regularly right now?" If your answer is no, then when are you going to start? If you are truly committed to becoming one of the best producers in your company or industry, then make that commitment today and stop looking for an easier way out. There is none. However, I guarantee that if you do put in the time and effort as I've indicated here, your career and your life will change in exciting and fulfilling ways. And believe me, the positive changes that result are worth many times over the relatively small effort you will put in.

HOW TO USE ASSUMPTIVE STATEMENTS

Want to make your presentations instantly better? Then invest some time and change your closed-ended, weak closing statements and questions into powerfully persuasive, assumptive statements that lead your buyer to make the decision you want them to make. Assumptive questions are just that—they assume an answer rather than ask for it, and in doing so, they cut through any hesitation or resistance a prospect is tempted to put up. Also, a good assumptive question also heads off any smokescreen objection a prospect might try to hide behind.

If you look at your presentation carefully enough, you will find many opportunities to replace closed-ended questions with assumptive ones. Here are some examples to get you started:

Change: "Do you have any questions for me?"

To: "What questions do you have for me?"

Change: "Would you like to get more business?"

To: "How much more business would you like to get?"

Change: "Do you think you would get more traffic (or leads) from using this?"

To: "How much more traffic (or leads) do you think you would get using this?"

Change: "Do you think your other (departments/locations/and so on) could benefit from this?"

To: "How many other (departments/locations/and so on) would benefit from this?"

Change: "Do you have a budget for this?"

To: "What kind of budget do you have for this?"

Change: "Do you think your partner/manager/corporate would agree with this?"

To: "Why do you think your partner/manager/corporate would agree with this?"

Change: "Does this make sense to you?"

To: "Tell me, what part of this makes the most sense to you?"

Change: "Is this something you would like to go ahead and try?"

To: "Let's go ahead and get you started...."

Change: "What do you think your manager will say?"

To: "How do we get your manager to say yes to this?"

Change: "Are you the ultimate decision maker on this?"

To: "And besides yourself, who else would be making the final decision on this?"

Change: "Is your [current solution] providing all the leads you need?"

To: "What would you like to most improve with your [current solution]?

As you can see, nearly any open-ended question can be turned into an assumptive one. And do you see how much more suggestive and powerful they are? Go through your qualifying scripts, your closing scripts, and your rebuttal scripts, and look for opportunities to transform your closed-ended questions into powerful and effective assumptive ones. Then watch as you gain more control over selling situations and begin eliminating the objections and stalls that you may be creating right now.

THE IMPORTANCE OF CONFIRMING YOUR ANSWERS

Let me give you a quick, easy-to-use technique that will make your closes shorter and more effective. The technique is to confirm your answers to any buying question—or any objection—that you get. The importance of this came up for me while I was listening to a series of phone calls during which a sales rep was conducting a demo of a product. When the prospect asked the price, the rep gave it to him, but then he just kept talking to justify it!

It went something like this:

Prospect: "So how much does this cost?"

Closer: "The price for set-up in your location is $700, and then the monthly fee is $125 a month. Of course, we do a lot for you for that set-up fee. It takes our tech staff... And that monthly fee also covers... We also ... and another feature with this is ... "

What happened on this call is that the closer, in his attempt to justify the price, actually introduced a series of questions that turned into objections, and that led to this sale being stalled. That is the big danger whenever you begin *talking past the close*.

What the rep should have done is use a confirmation statement to see how the price sounded for the prospect. Something like this:

Prospect: "So how much does this cost?"

Closer: "The price for set-up in your location is just $700, and then the monthly fee is just $125 a month. Does that work for you?"

If building more value was required, then he could have gone into a brief explanation of that, but even after that he would still have to confirm his answer (which he and most other closers rarely do).

To take this further, if the prospect then said that it did fit within his budget, the next question would have been:

"And how well do you think this will work in your company?"

If the answer to that question was positive, then:

"Great! Then let me show you how to get started...."

This way, the close could have happened long before the rep talked his way past the sale.

This idea of confirming your answer is crucial not just when you answer a question, but also when you answer an objection as well. For example, after you answer a price objection, or objection about availability or any other objection, the thing to do is confirm your answer. Use any of the following:

"Did I answer that for you?"

"Is that more clear now?"

"Does that make sense to you?"

"Do you see now why we charge for that?"

If you get a yes, or if you get buy-in, then you ask for the order! Say:

"Great, then let me show you how easy it is for you to get started with this...."

If the prospect then has another question or objection, you answer that as well, confirm your answer, and ask for the order—over and over again.

The point here is that if you confirm your answer, then it is time to ask for the order again. If you don't, and you are probably talking or pitching after you answer a question and, chances are, you will be talking past the close. And why would you want to do that?

SEVEN THINGS TO SAY WHEN PROSPECTS DON'T HAVE THE TIME FOR YOUR PRESENTATION

We have all been there. You call your prospect back at the appointed time for your presentation, and they tell you any of the following:

"This isn't a good time."

Or

"I only have a few minutes."

Or

"How long will this take?"

Or

They tell you they have a meeting in 10 minutes, can you give them the information anyway? Or any other put-off that will cut short the 30-minute comprehensive presentation you had planned.

Most sales reps respond to these objection-like receptions by asking if they would prefer to set another time. That response might be appropriate with the first put-off—the "This isn't a good time,"—but with any of the others, I have a better technique for you.

Let's start at the beginning. First, when you get this kind of response from a prospect you qualified a week or so ago, don't be surprised! Face it: it is a law in all sales—*leads never get better!* If you sent out the hottest lead ever, a 10 on a scale of 1 to 10, then when you call them back, have you ever noticed that now they're about a 7–8?

And of course since most sales reps don't qualify thoroughly enough, most of the leads they stuff into their pipeline are made up of 5s and 6s. And you can imagine how *they* are when reps reach them. So expect that your leads are going to drop in interest and receptiveness when you call them back, and then be prepared with a best-practice approach to handling this. Here is what to do.

Whenever a prospect responds to your call to do a presentation with one of the preceding responses, the "How long will this take?" kind of response, don't offer to call them back later. Instead, get them to reveal their true level of interest to you, and get them to tell you exactly how to pitch them to get the deal. Here are a number of statements you can use to do just that:

"I can take as long or as little time as you need. Let's do this: Why don't you tell me the top three things you were hoping to learn about this, and I'll drill right down and cover those areas for you. What's number one for you?"

Or

"Absolutely, we can do this pretty quickly. Tell me, what would you like to know most about how this might work in your environment?"

Or

"I understand. It sounds like I caught you at a bad time. Let's do this: If you needed to see or learn just one thing about this to determine if it will work for you, what would that be?"

Or

"No problem. Our presentation is pretty in-depth, but I can do this. Go ahead and tell me two things that are absolute deal breakers for you, and I will see if we pass the test. Then if we do, we can schedule some more time later to go into detail on how the rest works. Fair enough?"

Or

"In 10 minutes, I can show you some things that will help you determine whether or not you would like to spend more time with me later. In the meantime, let me ask you: What would you need to see the most to say yes to this?"

Or

"I understand. We are all busy. Let me just ask you: Has anything changed since we last spoke?"

(Now *really* listen.)

Or

"Tell you what: let's reschedule something for later when you have more time, but in the ten minutes we have right now, let me ask you some questions to determine whether this would still be a good fit for you...."

(Now thoroughly requalify your prospect.)

As you can see, the preceding responses are all aimed at getting your prospect to reveal to you both their level of interest and what it is going to take to sell them—or whether or not they are still a good prospect for you. Also, these prepared responses help you reestablish control of the call. Have some fun with these. Customize them to fit your personality or the personality of the person you are speaking with. Find your favorites and then, as always, practice, drill, and rehearse them until they become your automatic response when your prospect tells you they don't have time for your presentation.

HOW TO STAY ORGANIZED (AND EFFICIENT!)

How are you at organizing your day? Do you find that the "small things" like organizing your office, organizing your laptop, checking in with old customers just to see how they are doing, distract you from what you know you need to be doing to make more money—that is, cold calling, following up on leads, calling prospects back who are on the fence, and so forth?

If you are like most inside sales reps, then there are many distractions that seem to scream out for your time and attention. There is checking and responding to emails, organizing your calling campaign and leads, keeping your leads and notes together and up to date in Salesforce, and calling on existing customers to follow up on sales. There are also meetings, social network research, websites and prospect research on Facebook, and so on. When it is finally time to prospect for new business, it is lunch time, or time to go home!

On top of all of that (or perhaps at the bottom of it all), there is the real dread of making those outbound prospecting calls—you know, call reluctance. So what can you do to break out of this vicious cycle of procrastination?

You are going to use the proven time management technique known as "The Top Three Priorities." Here is how it works. First, before you go home for the day, make a list and identify the three most important things you need to do the next day to accomplish the only goal that matters: Making sales. These items might include:

- Call the hottest prospects in your pipeline—those most likely to buy that day.

- Make a definite number of cold calls to keep your pipeline full.

- Follow up with recent orders to upsell them.

- Reach a certain number of existing clients to look for upsell opportunities.

- Put together proposals or quotes.
- Follow up on proposals or quotes.
- Check in with prospects or leads in your pipeline.

Once you have picked out the *three* most important items that you can do the next day, pick again the three next most important items that are going to lead to sales that day and write these down in order of importance and leave them on your desk for the next morning.

By the way, making this list the night before is crucial, as it allows your subconscious mind to begin devising ways of accomplishing them for you. Believe it or not, what you write down and intend to do sends a powerful message to your subconscious mind, and it will work hard during the evening and night, preparing you to accomplish your goals for the next day.

Now here is the key to the whole process of identifying your Top Three Priorities. When you get in the next day, start working on one priority at a time and work through it to completion *before* you move on to the next one. In other words, resist the temptation to multitask these three priority items. As you know, if you begin doing too many things at once, you end up not completing any of them.

The key to this powerful time-management technique is to pick out the *most important* priority you have identified, then complete it, and *then* move on the next one, complete that one, and then move on to the next one and complete that as well. If something comes up—like an inbound customer call, or an urgent email you need to address—then certainly handle that, but then immediately get back to the priority you are working on.

While I know that many other things will compete for your attention, and some of them might even need to be done, sticking with and accomplishing your Top Three Priorities will not only make you ultra-efficient, it will relieve a lot of anxiety for you as well. Let me give you a brief example.

Years ago when I decided to become a full-time consultant, I had a lot of work to do on my business. I had to create the website, write all the copy for the pages, create downloadable e-books for my initial products, find hosting sites, shopping carts, write e-zines, create opt-in pages and links, deal with my webmaster several times a day, proof all the pages endlessly, and much, much more. While all these projects were critical for me to begin my consulting practice (and I enjoyed doing them), what I found after a while was that I had stopped doing the things that brought me the money. I needed to pay my mortgage and my webmaster, and so on. In other words, I had stopped cold calling and selling. The solution to this was to create my Top Three Priorities list and make sure that I worked through them, one by one, before I responded to my webmaster, before I began proofing pages or writing copy, before I created another web page, and so on.

I started by making 35 cold calls each day. I took all the time I needed to make these calls, and only *after* I was done I then follow up with any leads I had (priority number two). When I finished that, *then* I moved on to my next priority—which was to call five people in my network to prospect for work or to get other leads from them. Only after I completed all three of these priorities did I dive into my work on the business. What I found reinforced the importance and effectiveness of this time management technique.

The first benefit was that as I took care of the important and difficult things—like cold calling—I felt great relief because that big pressure was lifted from me. Second, as I completed the next priority, I gained confidence and encouragement as I scheduled meetings and moved closer to closing deals. Finally, as I worked through the last priority, I felt a tremendous sense of freedom and accomplishment, because I knew that the things that would have nagged at me all day were completed. I was now free to handle the other important things guilt-free!

Another benefit started showing up as well: I started closing deals and making money. As the saying goes: "Sales solve everything." It did make all the work on the business and website so much easier. As I continued to set three priorities and complete them one by one each day, I made significant progress both on my career and on my website. The rest, as they say, is history.

But it all started by setting and working through each of my three priorities, one by one, before I moved on to all the other important things that tugged at me in my day. If you are struggling to take back control of your day, then pull out a piece of paper and start writing down your Top Three Priorities right now. Remember to organize them around your most important goal for each day: *making sales*. This one technique is the most important time management strategy I have ever learned, and I guarantee that once you begin using it, you, too, will feel more confident, become more efficient, and make more sales.

How to Get Your Prospect Talking

Have you ever had a prospect that you just can't read? Someone who, during your closing presentation, simply won't share much of his or her opinion one way or the other? Or should I ask how many prospects do you have like that? These days, many prospects hide behind nebulous stalls like, "Let me think about it," or "I'll run this by the committee," and so forth, and it is often hard to know where they stand. Then it gets worse when you try to set an appointment to get back with them only to hear, "Let me get back to you."

If you are struggling with prospects like this, then it's time to learn some advanced closing skills that only the Top 5 Percent are comfortable using. And that means asking open-ended questions and encouraging your prospect to be honest and to fully answer your questions either negatively or positively. While this may sound easy to do, only the top pros know how to fully listen long enough for their prospect to tell them how they really feel. (They use their mute button!) Top pros are not afraid of getting a negative response. They are interested instead in what the prospect is really thinking.

To get your prospect to open up, you need some well-crafted scripts that lead your prospect into telling you the truth. Then it is up to you to adapt and make them your own so you can deliver them sincerely and not sound sales-y. Take some time to review the choices that follow and do just that—make them your own.

Ask Open-Ended Questions

Open-ended question 1:

> "You know, _____, we all buy emotionally and go with our gut feelings. Share with me: What is your gut telling you is good about our solution, and what is it telling you isn't so good?"

(Now hit mute and listen—same advice after each rebuttal.)

Open-ended question 2:

"_____, I'm sure you are weighing this purchase against some of our competitors so tell me, in what ways are we better than your next option, and in what ways are we weaker?"

Open-ended question 3:

"_____, you have probably heard of the old Ben Franklin way of making a decision haven't you?"

(Wait for a response.)

"Ben would make a list of all the reasons to make a decision to move forward with something, and all the reasons not to. If the reasons were stronger to move forward, he would.

So tell me, what are the reasons, as you see them, for moving forward with this, and what are the reasons not to?"

Open-ended question 4:

"_____, I know there are other people who need to weigh in on the final decision on this, so tell me, if you had to put a wager on it, would you bet that there were more votes on moving forward on this or more votes against it?"

Layer:

"And why is that?"

Open-ended question 5:

"Now, _____, I know you like what we have, and there are probably some things you don't like. Tell me, if we could deliver more of what you *do* like, what would that be?"

Layer:

"And if we could give you less of what you don't like, what would *that* be?"

Then,

"And why is that?"

Open-ended question 6:

"_____, some people love our solution and some people—believe it or not—not so much. Tell me, what do you *love* about us, and what about this is making you hesitate right now?"

As you can see, these scripts are designed to get someone who is noncommittal to begin opening up and to tell you where they stand—both positively and negatively. Once you know where someone is emotionally and logically with your product or service, you will have the leverage to adjust your close and get closer to a sale.

SOFTENING STATEMENTS THAT KEEP PROSPECTS TALKING

One of the objections I always get from salespeople who don't want to use scripts is that they are afraid they will sound so, well, scripted. I tell them that if they sound like they are reading them, then of course they will. But if they internalize them and then deliver them naturally, then they don't sound like scripts at all. Instead, they will sound confident and professional.

The other objection I get about using scripts is that many scripts sound very sales-y. Some even sound too direct and pushy. Again, it is all about how you deliver them. For example, are you matching the pacing of the person you are speaking with? Are you using timing properly? Are you hesitating and adding the right inflection at the right time?

You see, the great thing about scripts is that they afford you greater flexibility in not only what you say, but more important, how you say it. Let's face it: inflection, pacing, and tone are everything when you are selling over the phone.

The other great thing about a carefully crafted and delivered script is that you can use softening statements if you sense your prospect is getting irritated, or short, or is in a hurry. If you have to ask for some sensitive information—like who your competition is, or what their budget is, or how they figure into the decision-making process—you can preface your question with a softening statement to help bring the defenses of a prospect down, and to make yourself sound more natural and more real.

Here are a variety of softening statements you can weave into your opening and closing scripts to help you connect with your prospect and to get them talking.

For Opening Scripts

Softening statement 1:

> "If you don't mind me asking, can you tell me, roughly, what you paid for that previously?"

Softening statement 2:

> "And _____, obviously you are going to run this by others there. Do you mind me asking how you figure into the final decision process?"

Softening statement 3:

> "_____, don't take this the wrong way—and I'm only asking to know for comparison purposes—but when you got [X product or service] the last time, what did you end up paying for that?"

Softening statement 4:

> "_____, the only reason I'm asking is that if you purchase [more than the normal amount or add on to the order], then I may be able to offer you a discount. Hey, we all like to save money, right?"

Softening statement 5:

> "_____, I don't want to go above your head, but I also don't think it is fair for you to do my job for me—so do you mind if I ask if it's okay to speak with [the boss] briefly and answer any questions he has directly?"

Softening statement 6:

"_____, do you mind if I ask you just a couple of quick questions to see whether or not this might be a good fit for you?"

Softening statement 7:

"I promise I won't take a lot of your time—I know you're busy. Can I ask how long you have....?"

Softening statement 8:

"I don't know about you, but I usually hate talking to salespeople I don't know. Just so I can be respectful of your time, do you mind if I ask you...."

Softening statement 9:

"_____, you and I haven't spoken yet, and I hate to barge into your day, so do you mind if I take just two minutes to see if this is something you would like to learn more about?"

For Closing Calls

Softening statement 1:

"Before I show you all the ins and outs of this, do you mind if I ask you again: What specifically are you hoping to learn today?"

Softening statement 2:

"Our price for this is $_____. Do you mind if I ask how that compares with what you are spending now for all of this?"

Softening statement 3:

"_____, I know you want to think about this and that makes perfect sense. Do you mind if I just get an idea of what part of this is not resonating with you right now?"

Softening statement 4:

"_____, please don't think I am being too forward here, but after we are done and you have learned everything about this, is it fair that I ask you for a simple yes or no?"

Softening statement 5:

"_____, would you mind if I asked you: 'If the price on this was closer to what you felt comfortable spending, would this be the solution you would want to go with?'"

Softening statement 6:

"I totally understand. Believe me, I do. Besides that, though, what else might be standing in the way of you saying yes to this?"

Softening statement 7:

"Hey, I get it. You have options and you want to talk to others. But let me ask you: From what we have just gone over and from what you understand about this today, are we even in the ballpark for earning some of your business?"

Softening statement 8:

"_____, if at any time this isn't sounding like it is for you, would you be willing to let me know?"

Softening statement 9:

"_____, what I don't want to do is talk your ear off. So please do me a favor. If you have heard enough and it sounds like you have, would you let me know?"

Softening statement 10:

"_____, do you mind me asking why you are still considering other companies for this?"

Softening statement 11:

"_____, I know you have a lot of options out there. Would it be okay for me to ask you what the deciding factors will be for you?"

Softening statement 12:

"_____, you know we are not for everyone, and if we're not for you that's okay. Obviously, I would like your business, but I would rather you do what you think is right for you. Do you mind telling me what you are really thinking about right now?"

Softening statement 13:

"Is there anything I can say or do to get you to reconsider?"

Softening statement 14:

"_____, I know we are not the cheapest option out there—and there are reasons for that—but is it just the price on this or are there others things keeping you from saying yes to this?"

Softening statement 15:

"I know I've given you a lot of information on this. Could you give me an indication of where you are leaning?"

As you can see, many of these responses are down-to-earth and real-world responses—something you might say to a friend or family member. The more real you are, the more your prospects will feel it, and the more they will be honest with you and reveal what it might take for them to move forward with you.

POSITIVE STATEMENTS THAT HELP YOU SELL

When I began my sales career all those years ago, I was told that at the bottom of all successful sales was a transfer of emotion. My manager told me that I was either transferring my positive feelings about my product onto my buyer, or he or she was transferring their negative feelings about it to me. Whoever could transfer more of their emotion and feeling would sway the other.

Now that may seem a bit simplistic to you, but if you look at the essence of it, there is a lot of truth to it. You have probably heard some of the sayings like, "Enthusiasm sells!" or, "Whoever has the strongest reasons to buy or not buy usually wins," and things like that. My question to you is: "Are you enthusiastically presenting your product or service on every call?"

I am sure you know the difference between having a good day and having a bad day, right? Have you ever noticed how pumped up you are right after a big sale? You are positive, on top of the world, unstoppable, right? This is why good sales managers always tell their reps to "get back on the phone" after they write a deal. Have you ever noticed how objections aren't quite so bad when you are in such a positive mood?

The converse is true as well, isn't it? Have you ever noticed how, when you are having a bad day, it is easy to be put off when cold calling and how you don't pitch with quite the same level of enthusiasm and belief? Maybe you have even given up after being put off or after an objection, only to then say something like this to yourself: "Well, this just isn't my day. Maybe I should just stop calling today and try again tomorrow?" If you are in sales, then I bet you can relate to both of these scenarios, can't you?

What I have found over the years is that most salespeople let their prospect's mood affect and lead theirs rather than the other way around. After listening to thousands of calls over the years, I can hear how a sales rep's voice drops or slumps as soon as a prospect cuts them off or tells them they don't have much time, or worse, that they don't really see the value in their product or service.

Top reps, have a different approach. They know that it is their job to transfer their belief and attitude to their prospects, and they stand ready with a list of Power Statements that help get their prospect into the proper mindset. They then overwhelm them with their positive attitude and don't give up until they get the sale.

Here are a few statements you should have ready at all times when you are closing or cold calling. Any one of these can mean the difference between who catches whose attitude and who sells who.

Use Power Statements

Positive statement 1:

"_____, once you truly understand how this works, you will be as impressed as I was during my interview here. Let me take just a moment to fill you in...."

Positive statement 2:

"_____, I guarantee you will be 100 percent happy if you take just a moment with me to show you what this can do for you...."

Positive statement 3:

"Are you ready to be amazed today? Because after I show you the changes we have made to this (product or service), you will be more than surprised. Go ahead and open that...."

Positive statement 4:

"_____, virtually nothing that you know about this (product or service) has remained the same. In fact, we have made every part of it better and added some features that you will soon never be able to live without. For example...."

Positive statement 5:

"I'm sure you wouldn't mind learning why we are the bestselling [your product or service] in the marketplace, so let's do this—go ahead and open that email and let me point out just two things that make us number one...."

Positive statement 6:

"_____, you do want to go with the best company you can for this with the best customer support and loyalty program, don't you?"

Positive statement 7:

"_____, I couldn't wait to speak with you today. I've just had an update that will knock your socks off! Do me a favor and grab that brochure...."

Positive statement 8:

"_____, I couldn't wait to speak with you today! So much good news has happened since we last spoke that I don't even know where to begin. Tell you what, let's start by reviewing that email I sent you...."

Positive statement 9:

"_____, there are three things that make me excited to come to work every day, and they also make all my clients excited to sign up with us. The first is...."

Positive statement 10:

"_____, are you ready to finally get the best [your product or service] on the market today? If so, then grab a pen and get ready to take some notes. I've got some exciting things to tell you today...."

If Prospect Is Negative

Positive statement 1:

"If that were true, I wouldn't be representing this. The fact is, most people don't fully understand how this works, but once they do, they understand why we are the number one product on the market. Let's do this...."

Positive statement 2:

"Let me tell you just three reasons why we are the number one brand in this industry, and if you still aren't interested after that, then we will part as friends. The first is our world-class customer support...."

As you can see, by using these kinds of statements, you are the one setting the tone of the call. Never forget that enthusiasm *does* sell, and always check your attitude before you pick up the phone. And have these statements ready!

HANDLING OBJECTIONS WHEN REQUALIFYING

As I have suggested before, it is always a good idea to requalify your prospect at the start of your demo or presentation. Doing so allows you to anticipate objections and position your presentation to speak to whatever resistance you may face later. And to take it a step further, it is also a good idea to use a trial close with the right prospects in the right situations. When I make this suggestion, I get a lot of pushback from sales reps. "But if I ask for the deal before I have given the presentation, before I have given the value, they will just say no!" is the most common objection I get.

So let me make it clear: you are not asking for the deal at the beginning; instead, you are using a trial close to access the next steps and to get a feel for the kind of pushback you might get at the end of your demo. Getting this information is crucial for you, and you can leverage this information during the rest of the call.

Using Trial Closes

There are several ways to use a trial close. There is the aggressive way (here) that is appropriate if you have been aggressive on the first call and identified the decision maker and time frame. If you have, then something like this can be appropriate:

Trial close 1:

"_____, as we talked about last week, I am going to go through everything now, answer any questions you have, and if, at the end of the demo today, you feel this will definitely help you drive more business, then is this something you can put to work for you today?"

Some sales reps (okay, most sales reps) will be uncomfortable with this kind of trial close because they have not done a thorough enough job of qualifying up front. If that is the case, then here is a softer trial close:

Trial close 2:

"_____, I'm looking forward to covering everything with you today. Just out of curiosity, if at the end you feel this is just what you are looking for, what would be the next steps to putting it to work for you?"

This is a soft, nonthreatening way of finding out what his or her answer is going to be at the end when you ask for the sale. All of you have to agree you would like to know that, right?

And here is an in-between way of using a trial close at the beginning:

Trial close 3:

"_____, at the end of today's demo, if you like what you see, is there anything that would prevent you from putting this to work for you in the next two weeks?"

The positive way of asking this is:

Trial close 4:

"_____, at the end of today's demo, if you like what you see, is this something you could put to work for you in the next two weeks?"

How to Handle Resistance

These are some of the ways of using a trial close at the beginning of your presentation. Now what happens if you get pushback? Here is how to handle that. If your prospect says:

"I am not ready to make a decision."

(Or any variation of that, you simply respond with the following.)

Handling resistance 1:

"That is no problem, and I'm not asking you to. We haven't gone through the benefits here nor have I answered any of your questions. All I am trying to get a feel for is *if* you like what you see and you think there is value here for you and your company, what would you have to do to get this approved?"

Handling resistance 2:

"I'm with you and don't mistake my question for pressure. All I am asking is *if*, after the end of our demo today, you see value here and want to pursue this, what are the next steps on your end?"

What you are trying to do is isolate and uncover what the objection or stall is going to be at the end so you can position yourself to deal with it and advance the sale. For example, if your prospect then says something like:

"I'll have to take it to the committee."

(Or show it to the boss, and so forth, then you isolate this with the following.)

Handling resistance 3:

"I understand and most people I speak with do as well. Tell me, if you really like this, though, what kind of influence do you have in that process?"

Handling resistance 4:

"I'm with you. And if you *are* in favor of this, how would that affect their decision?"

How to Close

Again, you want to isolate the objection and understand the stall so you can deal with the close at the end of your presentation better. For example, if your prospect tells you they *do* have influence, then at the end of your demo, this is how you close:

Closing statement 1:

"So, does this sound like something you feel is the right fit?"

(Get buy-in here, then)

"Great, then what can I do to help them agree with us?"

See how this goes.

If the objection or stall at the beginning of your demo is the "no budget" stall, then say:

Closing statement 2:

"Please, I'm not asking you to invest in this right now, and we can deal with where you would get the budget from later. All I want to know now is that *if* you found value here and were determined to move forward, is there a way you could find the resources? Again, if you were convinced?"

If the answer is no, then you need to deal with the money issue now rather than spend the next 45 minutes on a demo that will end with the same objection! I know this isn't going to be a popular answer for many of you—again, I know you would rather pitch until you are blue in the face—but if your prospect cannot afford to do it at the end, why would you want to?

What I am suggesting here is what I have taught for many years, and what I personally do now when closing on my training services. I start by properly qualifying prospects upfront—on the cold or prospecting call—on the six qualifiers (which I have written about extensively elsewhere—check out my blog if you missed it: http://mrinsidesales.com/insidesalestrainingblog. Then I requalify *before* I waste the time and effort of giving a long pitch to someone who isn't or won't buy at the end.

Doing this will make you a more successful closer and confident closer as well.

ALWAYS HAVE THIS CLOSE HANDY

How many times do you get the objection, "Let me talk to my (partner, boss, manager, spouse, and so on)"? In any kind of sale, this is one of the most common objections or stalls prospects use. They use it because sales reps don't seem to have any effective comeback for it.

Instead, how many sales reps respond actually creates another stall and can actually lose the sale for them! This objection is so common, that it has spawned the following variations.

"Let me run this by...."

Or

"I'll have to get with...."

Or

"Let me check with...."

Or

"I'll show this to my boss and see what he wants to do...."

I am going to give you the right rebuttal to this and give you a real-life example of how I used this rebuttal—and what I learned—just this week while I was closing a prospect on one of my training programs.

I was speaking with a customer who had recently purchased one of my books of phone scripts. I had never spoken to her before, but decided to call her to learn how the scripts were working out for her. During our conversation, I learned what her company was about, what they sold, and how many reps they had. I also established that she was one of the owners. After listening to exactly what she was trying to accomplish, I suggested helping her by writing customized scripts and having her team record those sales presentations so I could revise and perfect their scripted sales approach. I also added that these recordings could then be used as a "training library" that she could use to onboard new hires. Then I asked how that sounded.

That is when I got the preceding objection. She said: "I'll run this by my partner...."

This is where 80 percent of sales reps let the prospect go with, "Okay, when should I follow up?" *That is the wrong response to make.* Instead, the proper technique is to isolate this objection by taking the other decision maker out of the equation so you can gauge how your prospect truly feels about it. Because let's face it: if your prospect isn't sold, then the other decision maker isn't going to be, either. So here is the close you need here. I said to her:

> "That's great. Definitely show it to your partner. And let me ask you: If your partner says it sounds good, what would you tend to do then?

And this is where this technique really pays off. If she had said, "I'd do it!" then I would have set some coaching times on our calendars (nothing set in stone; just set some tentative dates—another form of a trial close), but if she said what she did, then I would know exactly where I stood. She said, "I'd then go back to my reps and tell them to use the scripts I just bought and see how that goes first. I'd tell them I had already spent a lot of money on them and they needed to produce before I'd be willing to spend more."

How is that for a good answer? You are probably thinking, "Good answer? But Mike, it doesn't sound like she is going to buy!"

And that is okay. I would much rather know now than fool myself into thinking that she will speak with some mythical "other" decision maker who will persuade her to buy. It doesn't happen that way! She already had her answer, and now I do, too. Remember—some will, and some won't. Who's next?

You see, what is so good about this technique, and her honest answer to it, is that she revealed that she isn't going to be a sale. That means I get to move on. Compare this to how most sales reps would just schedule a call back and then begin chasing her. How many of these types of unqualified leads currently clog up your pipeline?

When I say this is the type of close to always have handy, I mean it. Every time you find yourself in this situation, always, always, isolate this objection/stall to find out where you really stand. It will save you tons of time (and frustration), and you can spend that time prospecting and finding real buyers rather than chasing prospects who have no intention of ever buying from you.

THE THREE TIMES TO HANDLE AN OBJECTION

Most sales reps hate getting objections. When they get them, their hands start to sweat, their heart takes the elevator down into the pit of the stomach, and they start wishing they had gotten that graduate degree and avoided sales altogether. Ever had days like this?

This is how many sales reps react when they get objections, but not the top producers. Top producers view and react to objections very differently. To start with, because top producers thoroughly qualify their prospects up front they generally uncover and deal with many objections during the qualifying stage. Objections like, "I'll have to show this to my partner," and others are already known and in many cases eliminated. (See previous sections on proper qualifying, specifically, scripts like, "And after the presentation, if you think this will work for you, what would the next steps on your end be?" and so on.)

Also, top producers have taken the time, long in advance, of scripting out two or three different rebuttals to the objections they get, so if they do get them, they know exactly what to say to overcome them. In other words, they are rarely caught off guard because they know what to say to deal with them.

Third, because top producers know what the objections or stalls are likely to be in advance, and since they are prepared for them with solid scripts and techniques to overcome them, they can take advantage of the timing of "when" to handle an objection. Unlike most sales reps who feel they have to handle an objection the moment they get one (and hence instantly lose control of the call), top producers realize that they have three options as to when to handle an objection.

1. The first time is when it comes up. Again, because top producers know what to say and how to effectively deal with objections, they have the choice of handling the objection when it comes up or of postponing it for later.

The first choice may be to handle the objection when it comes up. This is usually good if the prospect is rejecting a product or service at the beginning of the pitch because they haven't been through all the details (features and benefits) of the pitch yet.

The way to handle this is to use a script, of course. But the key is to handle the objection and then move back into the pitch. An example would be if a prospect objects to the price at the beginning. It could go like this:

Prospect: "This is out of our budget. The price is just too high."

(Or any other objection)

Rep: "You know it might seem that way now, but the price actually breaks down to about $2.00 per (lead, incident, and so forth), and when you look at it that way, it becomes very affordable—especially when you see how much time and effort it saves you. Let me just show you a couple of things...."

In this example, the rep answered the objection but instead of checking in with the prospect to see how the close landed, the rep instead kept control of the call by continuing with the pitch.

2. The second option to handling an objection is to postpone it until the end of the presentation. This is ideal if the prospect seems willing to keep listening but is stuck on an issue or two. This is especially appropriate if you know that you will cover this issue later in your presentation. The important thing here is to acknowledge that you heard the objection and promise to handle that at the end. It goes like this:

Prospect: "This is out of our budget...."

(Or any other objection)

Rep: "I can understand that, but let's do this. Before you make any decision on this, let's talk about all the things this can do for you first, and then you will be in a much better position to decide if this is worth it for you. I even have some payment options that might make the decision easier for you, as well.

"But first, let me show you this...."

What you are doing here is delaying answering the objection and thereby retaining control of the call. The nice thing about this is that by the end of your pitch, the prospect often won't even bring up the objection at all! You will be amazed by how often that actually happens once you begin using this technique.

In addition to this, if you know what the objection(s) are at the beginning of the pitch—or in the middle—you can begin pitching and building value around the known problem area (objection) in advance.

Postponing answering an objection like this is a great way to get your pitch in, keep control of the call, and prepare yourself for what you know might be coming at the end.

3. The third time to answer an objection is.... never! That's right. So many times, prospects will test you and try to put you off with many questions, stalls, and objections that it's just best to not respond at all. Here is how you do that:

Prospect: "This is out of our budget ... "

(Or any other objection)

Rep: "Some of our clients felt like that until they heard about...."

(Now give a benefit or two and keep pitching.)

This way, you've acknowledged the objection, but you remain positive and so sold on your solution that you let your enthusiasm drive the call—and often your prospect's mindset. It is said that enthusiasm sells, and that is true in many cases. The problem with most sales reps is that as soon as they hear an objection, they start to give up.

But by acknowledging the objection, remaining positive, and continuing with your pitch, you can often override any initial objection and get further into your pitch. In fact, if you have done this before, then you will often find that the prospect changes to a different objection the next time they bring one up!

These three times to handle an objection also work for questions as well. The important thing to remember is that it is up to you as to when to break your rhythm and deal with an objection.

The whole point is that *you* must remain in control of the call.

Try using the preceding techniques and scripts during your upcoming week of pitching your product or service. You will be amazed by how much easier your sale becomes—and how many more deals you'll get.

CHAPTER 8

How to Deal with Specific Objections

I know what you're thinking—"finally we get to specific rebuttals to objections!" Yes we do, but remember: many of these objections and stalls could have, and should have, been dealt with, uncovered, and even overcome during the prospecting call. If you do get them now at the end of your presentation, then I encourage you to use any of the specific, word-for-word closes below. As always, invest some time to customize them to fit your personality, product or service. And then make a commitment to practice, drill, and rehearse them so they become your automatic, go-to response. That way, if they do come up, you won't be rattled—rather, you'll be able to overcome them like top producers do.

HOW TO HANDLE "I HAVEN'T LOOKED AT THE INFORMATION YET"

Of all the objections sales reps get when they call a prospect back to close them, this is perhaps one of the most frustrating. And one of the big reasons is because it is usually caused by the sales rep! Here is what happens: sales reps send an email or brochure or link about their information out to a prospect, and when they call back, they invariably open the conversation with:

> "Hi, I'm just calling to see if you received the information I sent out to you?"

> *Or* worse:

> "Hi, just following up on the information I sent to you. Ah, did you have a chance to go through it yet?"

What do you think the prospect will say? Nine times out of 10, the prospect will give you the stall:

"I haven't looked at it yet...."

Then the sales rep is stuck and usually ends the call trying to reschedule a time to get back with them, and you can imagine how that goes.

So, the first tip is to stop asking *if* the prospect has received or read or gone through the information, and instead open your calls with this assumptive opening:

"Hi, _____, this is _____ with _____ calling about the information on our lead production process you wanted me to send to you. Now I'm sure you've gone through it a bit and probably have some questions for me. Just out of curiosity, what stood out to you the most?"

Then hit your mute button and begin listening to what they say, and how they say it. If at that time, they haven't gone through it yet, no problem! Just use any of the following responses to counter and move past this objection.

"I Haven't Looked at the Information Yet"

I haven't looked—Rebuttal 1:

"That's fine, in fact we can go over it together and this way I'll be able to answer any questions that come up for you. Can you open that email up for me? I'll be glad to hold while you do.

I haven't looked—Rebuttal 2:

"That's okay. I know you're busy, and it's actually a good thing you haven't looked at it yet. This way, while I'm on the phone with you, we can go through it together and I can answer any questions that come up. Do you happen to have it in front of you?"

Then use any of the following open-ended questions to engage the prospect:

"By the way, how are you currently handling your lead flow right now?"

Or

"You mentioned that you have compared these kinds of services before—what have you particularly been looking for in a new provider?"

I haven't looked—Rebuttal 3:

"I understand and that's okay. Let's do this: let's spend just a few minutes together right now, and I can direct you to a few points that might have particular interest to you. Go ahead and open that email/brochure up."

I haven't looked—Rebuttal 4:

"It sounds like you are as busy as me! No problem. Though let's do this: while I have you on the phone. Let me point a couple of things out to you so that later when you have more time to go through it, you'll know what to look for. Can you open that email briefly for me?"

I haven't looked—Rebuttal 5:

"That's okay. I know how busy you are. If you have just a minute now, I'll be happy to quickly point out some of the things that would appeal to you most. That will save you time later when you go through it. Do you have that handy?"

I haven't looked—Rebuttal 6:

"I'm sorry you didn't get it. It probably got stuck in your spam filter. Tell you what, I'll just go ahead and resend that right now. Okay, it's on the way to you. Tell me when you see it pop up."

I haven't looked—Rebuttal 7:

"I'll go ahead and send the brochure again, and while it's on the way to you, let me just ask you: "How motivated are you and your department to make a change in the way you handle....?"

Or

"And if you do like the program, besides yourself, who else would have to weigh in on this decision?"

(And any other requalification questions)

I haven't looked—Rebuttal 8:

"I completely understand, so how about this: go ahead and open that email up, and I'll just briefly point out two things that will give you a framework for when you do have time to go through it. Do you still have it in your inbox?"

I haven't looked—Rebuttal 9:

"Hey I get that all the time, so no worries. If you have just a few minutes now, I'd be happy to point a few things out. Can you open that email briefly for me?"

I haven't looked—Rebuttal 10:

"I completely understand and let's schedule a time when we can go over that together. How does later today or tomorrow morning look for you?"

As you can see, the best way to deal with the "I haven't had time to look at the information yet" objection is by not causing it to begin with! After that, if you do get this annoying stall, it's easy to sidestep it—if you know how. And now you do!

ELEVEN NEW WAYS TO HANDLE "THE PRICE IS TOO HIGH"

The price is too high is an objection that is as old has humanity itself. If you think hard enough, I am sure you can see the ancient Egyptians walking around an outdoor marketplace haggling with sellers using this very objection. And if you think even harder, you can probably envision weak sellers dropping their prices to make a sale. Things haven't changed much in four thousand years, have they?

The good news is that today there are a variety of proven ways to handle this age-old objection. The most obvious way is to see it for what it often is: a smokescreen hiding either a real objection or an attempt to have you to cave in and lower your price. In either of these situations the technique is to isolate the objection first and see what other stalls they come up with are before you negotiate price. You will see examples of these further on.

The following rebuttals are broken down into two groups: one set of rebuttals are for business-to-consumer sales—things like investments, insurance, home remodels, and so on—and the others are for business-to-business sales. In B to B, the objection often manifests more as a budgetary problem, but many times companies are looking for the best deal as well and so will still try to haggle on price with you.

The following are eleven new ways to handle both types of price and budget objections. Pick the ones you are most comfortable with and then make them your own and practice them until they become automatic. Given the frequency of this objection, you will be much more confident once you know how to handle them.

Business-to-Consumer Rebuttals

"The Price Is Too High—I Can't Afford That"

The price is too high—B to C 1:

> "I completely understand, and let's face it—we all have to work within a budget. But there is always a difference between a purchase and an investment. With a purchase, the value usually goes down, so regardless of what you spend—whether you can afford it or not—it's never going to appreciate or justify its value.

> "But with an investment—like this is—what you spend always justifies itself and ends up either saving you money in the long run or paying for itself month after month. And it always makes sense to invest in yourself, don't you agree?"

> (If yes)

> "Then here's what I recommend we do...."

The price is too high—B to C 2:

> "I definitely hear what you're saying, but let's take the price out of this for a moment and let me ask you: besides price, what other reasons do you have for not moving forward with this today?"

Note: I know this is a negative response, but given that you are trying to isolate the objection and uncover any others, in this case, it is recommended.

The price is too high—B to C 3:

> "I understand, and let me ask you: if price were not an issue on this—in other words, if this were more in alignment with what you could pay—is this something you would be interested in moving forward with today?"

> (If yes)

> "Great! Then tell me, where could you get the money from for this?"

The price is too high—B to C 4:

> "_____, you have probably heard that expression 'Other people's money,' right? Well, the good news with this is that you can use other

people's money to purchase this and begin enjoying the benefits right now! We have two ways for you to do that: You can either put this on a credit card and make whatever payments you can until it is paid off, or you can take advantage of our introductory offer where you can put no money down and make interest-free payments for as long as 18 months!

"In the meantime, you get to (start enjoying/the benefit/the protection) of this (service or product) from day one! Which of those two options do you like better?"

The price is too high—B to C 5:

"Now _____, for this investment—as with every other—you always have to ask yourself: What is working for me now and what could be working harder? Like all of us, I am sure you've got some stocks or funds that haven't performed quite as you had wished they would, don't you?

"Well this is your chance to move those underperforming investments around and put your money to work for you in a vehicle that can not only help you make up for lost time but exceed some of your better-producing investments. What comes to mind now that you wouldn't mind putting to better use for you?"

The price is too high—B to C 6:

"You know, you said something very important—you said that the price is too high. I'd really like to work with you on this, so help me to understand: What exactly are you comparing this price to?"

Business-to-Business Rebuttals

"The Price Is Too High—We Don't Have the Budget for It"

The price is too high—B to B 1:

"_____, I know we are not the cheapest out there—and it's important that you heard me right—we are not the 'cheapest' service on the market. There's a very important reason for that: the quality that you get with us goes far beyond the few extra dollars you'll invest today, and let me tell you the top three reasons why...."

The price is too high—B to B 2:

"And that's exactly why we offer our introductory package. Here's the thing: we're so convinced that you will come to appreciate the added services and value we offer that as soon as you begin using our service, you will forget all about the small initial cost.

"In fact, you will find that, in the long run, our (product or service) is not only affordable, but it saves you time *and* makes you money. And that's something you are interested in doing, isn't it?"

The price is too high—B to B 3:

"_____, if you really think about this from a business perspective, you will soon see that this is actually something that you can't afford *not* to do, and let me tell you why: if you don't put this (product or service) to work for you, while you may save a bit of money today, you will be losing money tomorrow in terms of (lost revenues, cost overruns, lost sales and opportunities, and so forth). As a business, you just can't afford to keep doing that.

"So here is what I recommend: do what all businesses do: finance this. Put it on your business credit card and make minimum payments, write off the interest, and all the while, begin profiting from the extra business and market share this will bring you. When you are ahead, just pay off the card and keep the profits from it! Let's go ahead and do this."

The price is too high—B to B 4:

"You know, a lot of business owners (VPs, etc.) at first think this is an expense, but think again: if it helps to bring you more business, and/or helps you keep the clients and customers you already have, then it becomes an investment in your success, doesn't it? And that is how all successful companies grow—they invest in their business.

"And that is what you have the opportunity to do right now. So let's get you started. . . ."

The price is too high—B to B 5:

"I hear you, _____, and let's just say that I could wave a magic wand and get you the money (or reduce the price to where it would fit within your budget). Level with me: What other reasons would you have for not at least considering putting this to work for you today?"

(Now listen for the *real* objection and deal with it appropriately.)

So now you have 11 new ways of handling the price objection. Make sure to listen for what the real objection is and then use the right script to overcome it.

SIX NEW WAYS TO HANDLE: "I NEED TO TALK TO MY BOSS"

The stall, "I need to speak with someone" is as old as "The price is too high" objection.

Despite it being around before all sales reps working today were born, many still have trouble overcoming it. You would think that with all the good rebuttals and techniques that have been written for it, reps might have figured it out, but alas, most reps still struggle with it.

To help you finally and definitively deal with it, I present you six new, improved, and proven ways of handling this stall. Now, let me make something clear: these techniques won't always work at overcoming this stall (many times they will, of course), but they *will* let you know how much of a stall this put-off is, whether it is a smokescreen, and how much of a shot you actually have at overcoming it, side-stepping it, or setting yourself up for a successful next call (or if there should even be a next call with a prospect!).

So let's start at the beginning. The first thing you need to do is qualify for this stall during your opening call. Do you? If you don't, then you are likely to keep getting this at the end of your presentations, and I know how frustrating that is for you. If you get it once, then shame on them, but if you keep getting it over and over again, then shame on you. To avoid this, here is what you must be asking on your first call:

"And _____, besides yourself, who weighs in on the final decision on something like this?"

And if they tell you their boss or corporate, and so on, then you must layer that with:

"And how much influence do you have in that?"

Layer:

"And what do they usually do when you bring them something like this?"

Layer:

"Based on what you know about how they feel about something like this, what do you honestly think they would do?"

You must get as much clarity as you can up front so you know what to expect when you go into your demo or presentation. And, of course, as you begin your close, you must also preface it with:

"Before we get started here, just so we're on the same page, if you like what you see at the end of our presentation today, what are the next steps for putting us to work for you at your end?"

Or—more aggressively:

"At the end of our presentation today, if you like what you see, can you put us to work for you today?"

Again, you must have clarity over the process before you begin your presentation. Once you have that, however, if you still get the "I'll have to show this to my partner, boss, and so on," then use one of the proven scripts that follow to handle it. As always, adjust them, customize them, and make them your own. Then practice, drill, and rehearse them until you have these responses down pat.

"I Need to Talk to My Boss/Partner/Corporate"

I need to talk to—Response 1:

"No problem, and are you going to recommend this to them?"

(If yes)

"Great! Then I'll hold on while you check with them...."

Or

"Great! And as you mentioned earlier, they do usually go with your recommendation, right?"

(If yes)

"Wonderful. Then I'll go ahead and get the paperwork started on my end. Can you reach out and see if they're available now to run this by them please?"

(Don't be fooled by the simplicity of this technique! About 20 percent of the time, the decision maker is sitting in the next room and some people will go and get the approval right then and save you valuable time in delaying and following up.)

I need to talk to—Response 2:

"I understand. Let me ask you two things: One, what do you think the biggest reason is they will put us to work for you today?"

(Listen for the buying motive.)

"And two: What do you think is the biggest reason they won't go with this solution?"

(Listen for what the real objection is and then layer and explore.)

I need to talk to—Response 3:

"Of course, and I understand. We talked before about your decision process. Let me ask you this, though: Is getting their approval the *only* thing holding us back from doing business together?"

(Listen carefully—if yes, then)

"Will you have time to talk to them before we next speak at 2:30 tomorrow afternoon? Great! Then because you are onboard with this, I will go ahead and prepare the paperwork. I'll email it to you, and I'll even reserve a spot for you."

(Give a brief pause here and wait for push back. If none)

"I'll look forward to us moving forward tomorrow!"

I need to talk to—Response 4:

"I understand, _____. Tell you what I'd be happy to do: I know *you* are behind this, right? Well, it's not fair to ask you to do my job, so if it's all right with you, I'll be happy to reach out to [decision maker] directly and answer any questions they might have. Would that be okay?"

(If no)

"No problem. Just out of curiosity, do you think they will go with this?"

(If no or don't know)

"What would it take for them to say yes?"

I need to talk to—Response 5:

"Well, I know you are behind this, and I know you need it—as we discussed during out first phone call. I know you have tried to sell something in the past yourself, and you have probably been told that someone had to 'talk to somebody else' before, right?

(Wait for a response.)

"Well, based on your experience, what do you honestly think is going to happen here?"

I need to talk to—Response 6:

"I understand, _____. I've been in sales a long time, and when someone tells me they have to speak with someone, it either means they really do or it means they don't really have to, and it's just a way to get me off the phone. I don't think that's happening here, but if it is, can you level with me?"

(If they really do have to speak with someone, then)

"Thanks for that. Now, based on what you know about this, and based on the fact that you would like to see us work together, what do you seriously think is going to stand in the way of this getting approved?"

Or

"Thanks for that. Now, based on what you know about this, and based on the fact that you would like to see us work together, what do you seriously think it is going to take to get this approved?"

There you have it! Six new ways to handle the "I need to speak with someone" objection.

Remember, some of these will help you overcome this stall, and even when they don't, they will usually help you smoke out the real objection. Once you get a handle on what is really likely to happen, then you can deal with it and overcome it—or move this prospect to the back burner and move on.

Ten New Ways to Handle the "I Need to Think About It" Objection

How do you currently handle it when your prospect gives you the stall, "I need to think about it"? If you are like most salespeople, you might give a wimpy, half-hearted response and then ask when you can call them back. That doesn't feel too good, does it?

Let's face it, whenever you get this objection—or any other stall that is similar to it, like, "I need to wait until next week/month," or "I'll get back to you"—you know as well as I do that it means your prospect is not yet sold and will probably not move forward with you. If you don't believe me, just look at your win/loss rate when you get this objection.

The way to handle this is to deal with it when it comes up and get your prospect to reveal what is *really* holding them back. The truth is, this objection (like so many) is usually just a smokescreen hiding the real objection. Use any of the following responses to get your prospect talking to you, to get them to reveal what is holding them back, and then you will have a chance to close the sale.

"I Need to Think About It"

I need to think about it—Response 1:

"_____, obviously, there is something that either doesn't make sense to you, or you need to check on something. I'm not sure which it is, but procrastinating on this won't help make this decision easier for you. Let me ask you this: What proof do I need to give you right now that this will work for you, to help you make that decision?"

I need to think about it—Response 2:

"You know, _____, whenever someone tells me they want to think about it, it is usually because the price isn't exactly where they would like it to be. Is that part of what you need to think about?

(If yes)

"Thanks for sharing that with me. Let me tell you why we price this the way we do, and what you get for that pricing."

(Break down each part of your product/service and justify/build value in your price. When done)

"You see, _____, you get what you pay for with this and then some. Let's go ahead and put this to work for you so you can start enjoying the benefits today...."

I need to think about it—Response 3:

"_____, I understand that thinking about it might make sense right now, but help me understand something. *What exactly* is holding you back from this today?"

I need to think about it—Response 4:

"_____, let me ask you: If I could email you testimonials from other clients that describe how much success they have had with this program, how much of a difference would that make for you right now?"

Listen carefully here. If this won't get them to move forward, then:

"Then, please—*I love to learn*—what specifically is holding you back from deciding on this today?"

I need to think about it—Response 5:

"_____, as you think about the reasons for either moving forward with this or not, I also want you to think about this: "How much has this been costing you each month by not getting it fixed?"

Layer:

"And tell me, how much time do you and your team spend on this each week?"

Layer:

"And how much more money could you (and your company/sales team/family) make if you finally found a solution that worked?"

And

"When you think about all the time and energy you have already spent thinking about this, how much has *that* cost you so far?"

And

"And if you continue to procrastinate, how much more do you think *that* will cost you?"

And

"If you went with our solution and it worked for you, how much would you save/make?"

Then

"As you can see, continuing to "think about this" has done nothing to fix it and it has only cost you time, money, and energy! So why don't you finally *do* something about this today and start reaping the rewards right now. Here's what we need to do. . . ."

I need to think about it—Response 6:

"I understand that you're not quite ready to decide on this. Out of curiosity, what factors do you still need to consider?"

Layer:

"And what kind of proof would you need to decide to go with us?"

Layer:

"And what else might hold you back from doing this with us?"

I need to think about it—Response 7:

"If there was one thing that would get you to say yes on this today, what would it be?"

I need to think about it—Response 8:

"_____, generally whenever I tell someone I need to think about it, one of three things is going on: one is that I am either weighing other options and want to make sure I am getting the best deal, or two what I am looking at just doesn't fit exactly what I need so I want to keep looking, or three it's too much money.

"Which of those three things is happening for you right now?"

I need to think about it—Response 9:

"_____, how much is a new customer worth to you?" [Listen carefully]

"And do you think what we are talking about here will bring you enough customers to at least pay for this?"

(If no, then they are not sold on your solution, and you will need to build more value.)

(If yes)

"Then there is no downside here for you and each additional client will simply make you money. So let's do this: let's sign you up for our introductory offer, and once you see how this *will* make you money we'll adjust your subscription to make you even more...."

I need to think about it—Response 10:

"_____, tell me two things: Why would you *not* do this, and why *would* you do this with me today?"

(Hit mute and let them talk.)

These rebuttals will work in a variety of situations if you take the time to customize them to your product or service, and then use them consistently. Ultimately, what you will find is that if you can get past this smokescreen to the real reason they are not moving forward with you, you will have the chance to either build value or clarify something they either don't understand or that they misunderstand. Once you do that, you will finally have a real shot at winning their business.

"I Want to Think About It"—Another 10 New Ways to Handle It!

I know, we just when through this objection! But sales reps always want more input on it, so here it is: the bottom line is that when someone says they want to think about it, *it means they aren't sold yet*. And it could very easily mean that they aren't sold on your solution, and they never will be because they have something else in mind.

Your job is to either uncover the hidden objection to learn what you need to do to overcome it, or get your prospect to reveal why they aren't going to go with your product or service. And that is why you must get your prospect talking. Now here is why this is so hard for salespeople: they don't want to ask because they don't want to know! Most sales reps would just prefer to let the prospect "think about it," hoping they will somehow persuade themselves to buy at some point in the future.

How often does *that* happen?

What usually happens is that the prospect then disappears never to be heard from again. And that is why sales reps dread this objection. But top producers know that getting their prospect talking at this point is crucial to finding out one of two things (and both of these things is a successful outcome, by the way):

1. What the hidden objection is, and finding a way of dealing with and overcoming it.

2. What the reason is they are not going to move on it, and being able to chalk this up as a learning experience and use the lessons to qualify the next lead better.

Let me repeat—*both* of these outcomes should be considered a success. The first because you will learn what you need to do to get the sale, and the second because you won't start chasing an unqualified lead that will never buy, plus you will learn how to not create another one in the future.

The following 10 rebuttals to "I want to think about it" are designed to get your prospect talking—and then you will be able to decide which category they go into.

Note: I would be remiss if I did not emphasize again that you should have avoided this objection from coming up in the first place by asking this type of qualifying question during your initial call: "And if you like what we have to offer, what would be your time frame for getting started?"

"I Want to Think It Over"

I need to think about it—Response 1:

"I understand. Just out of curiosity:

- "Do you understand exactly how the [explain the benefits of savings or making money here] works?"
- "And do you understand what we mean when we say, [stress any warranties/guarantees or customer service options]?"
- "Then while we are on the phone together, what other questions do you have?"

(If none)

"Then just to clarify my thinking, what part of this do you need to think over?"

I need to think about it—Response 2:

"Are you going to be thinking over the [name two or three benefits] we spoke about today or about whether this solution is the right fit for you?"

I need to think about it—Response 3:

"I know I've given you a lot to think about today. Do you mind me asking what part of this you'd like to think over?"

I need to think about it—Response 4:

"I understand, and I'm sure you have got other options to consider. Do you mind if I ask how we are stacking up to what you're also looking at?"

I need to think about it—Response 5:

"_____, it sounds like you are probably considering other options as well. Do you mind if I ask who else you're looking into?"

Layer:

"And how do we stack up compared to them so far?"

I need to think about it—Response 6:

"_____, besides yourself, who else is weighing in on this?"

Or

"Who else are you going to be thinking this over with?"

I need to think about it—Response 7:

"I totally understand. Many people I speak with want to consider all their options before making a decision. Tell me, who else is in the running for this?"

I need to think about it—Response 8:

"That's no problem. Level with me if you would, what would be holding you back from saying yes right now?"

Layer:

"And is this even a realistic option for you?"

I need to think about it—Response 9:

"And as you think about it right now, what would be the major reason for not moving forward with it?"

I need to think about it—Response 10:

"I understand. Not everyone I speak with is ready to move forward with it right away. Quick question: What would you need to see here for you to say yes to this?"

As you can see, all of these responses are geared toward getting your prospect to reveal what it is going to take for you to get the sale—and some are also geared to get your prospect to reveal why they will never be a deal.

Again, either way, you win.

How to Deal Effectively with the Influencer

So many closing situations now come down to pitching and trying to influence an influencer that it is time to teach the proper way of doing it. Let us start by identifying what an influencer is: an influencer is defined as someone who is involved in some way in the decision process—they either help make the decision, or they have to approve your product or service first before they pass it on to other decision makers, and so on. The bottom line, though, is there is always someone above your prospect who weighs in heavily or who has the final say on whether to move forward with you.

So the first thing you need to do is determine how your influencer fits into the decision process (if at all), and how much influence they do or do not have. Use the following questions during the qualification stage to determine this.

"And _____, besides yourself, who else would weigh in on this?"

Layer,

"And how does that process work?"

Layer:

"What is your role in that process?"

Qualify:

"And how much influence do you have in that process?"

Qualify:

"What generally happens when you recommend something like this? Do they generally go with your recommendation?"

Sometimes, you will be able to get through all these questions during the qualification stage, but if you get rushed, just ask as many as you can. It is important that you have a clear idea of what your influencer's role is, and how much influence he or she actually has before you go through your demo or presentation later.

By the way, once you begin your demo, it is always a good idea to go back through these questions before you launch into your pitch. Doing so will give you a heads up as to how it is likely to end. Wouldn't it be nice to know what the stall is before it even comes up? Once it does, here is how you handle it:

You: "So from what we've gone over, it sounds like this would be a great fit for you. Let's go ahead and get you started today."

Influencer: "Well, I'm going to have to show this to the committee."

You: "I understand, and just out of curiosity, based on what you've seen here today, do you personally think this would work for you [your company, department, and so on]?"

Influencer: "Yes, it looks good."

You: "Great, then I take it you are going to recommend it to the committee?"

Influencer: "Yes, I will."

You: "Good. Just out of curiosity, what generally happens when you take something to the committee that you personally recommend?"

Or

You: "Good. Just out of curiosity, when you take something to the committee that you personally recommend, what do they tend to do?"

Or

You: "Great! And how much influence do you have with what they will end up doing?"

Or

You: "Great! And how often do they go with your recommendation?"

Note: If you get buy-in that they generally go with what they recommend, then move to close:

You: "Wonderful! Since they usually take your recommendation, and since you are on board with this, here is what I recommend we do: I'll go ahead and get the contract out to you and schedule an install date. Once you get the approval, we'll already have much of the work done to get you going. Now, what is a good time for the installation?"

Let's break this down. The first thing you do (during the qualification stage) is to get clarity over how much influence your influencer actually has over the final decision. This is an important step that most salespeople miss.

Next, at the end of your close, you make sure that the influencer is sold on your product or service first, before you go down the "committee" path. It is crucial you get their buy-in at this stage.

After you do get their buy-in, this is when you can ask if they are going to recommend it and how much weight their recommendation carries. After that, you do a trial close on paperwork, and so on. You can make this as soft a trial close as you want. The point here is that you want to take your influencer as far as he or she will let you. The further they let you go, the more likely there will be a deal later.

Start implementing these techniques in your sales calls, starting with the qualification stage. The more you learn about the influencer and their role, the better equipped you will be to take the close further at the end.

CLOSING QUESTIONS TO ISOLATE THE OBJECTION

One of the most effective ways to deal with objections or stalls is simply to ask questions and isolate them. This works because many objections you get when closing are not actually objections at all—they are, instead, smokescreens hiding what the real reason or objection is. The reason sales reps have trouble with them is because they believe them and either try to overcome them or simply give up and opt to "call back later."

What you must do is get to the bottom of what is *really* holding a prospect back. Is it because they have a better deal elsewhere? Is it because they know their boss would never let them get a new product or service? Is it because they don't have the budget or because the price is too high? Is it because they aren't the real decision maker, or because they aren't qualified to make the decision on this at all? Is it because their current supplier or agent can always offer them a better price to keep their business? Is it because they don't know enough about how your product or service will really benefit them? Or is it because they think the learning curve will be too disruptive to their business? Is it because they do not believe in your value proposition? As you can see, there may be many things hiding behind a smokescreen objection. You get the idea.

There are many factors that might be standing behind the objection you are getting, and the only way to effectively overcome them is to know what the real or deciding factor is. You do that by questioning your prospect. Not in an interrogative way, but rather in a consultative way. You do it with layering questions and assumptive questions. You do it by using or adapting the questions that follow to fit your product or service and your personality.

Choose the following questions that feel right to you and then adapt them, post them in your cubicle, or record and listen to them until they become automatic for you.

Questions to Isolate the Objection

Isolating the objection—Question 1:

"_____, there is something that seems to be bothering you about this. Would you mind sharing with me what it is?"

Isolating the objection—Question 2:

"It sounds like there is something else that you would like to share with me about that. What else should I know about this?"

Isolating the objection—Question 3:

"What would you say is an example of why you need to think about this?"

Isolating the objection—Question 4:

"_____, help me to get an idea of what you are thinking about here...."

Isolating the objection—Question 5:

"Tell me what I need to know so I understand where you are with this?"

Isolating the objection—Question 6:

"What other vendors are you looking at for this?"

Isolating the objection—Question 7:

"What do you think is the biggest reason for not going with this now?"

Isolating the objection—Question 8:

"I totally get that you need to think about it. What one thing about this do you think you will need to think about the most?"

Isolating the objection—Question 9:

"You know, _____, it sounds like this is really important to you. Can you tell me why?"

Isolating the objection—Question 10:

"How does making a decision on this affect you or your department?"

Isolating the objection—Question 11:

"_____, what else do I need to know to get the full picture on this?"

Isolating the objection—Question 12:

"If you went with this and it didn't work out, how would that affect you?"

Isolating the objection—Question 13:

"If you go with this, and it works out, how will that affect you?"

Isolating the objection—Question 14:

"_____, just out of curiosity, how did you get to that?"

Isolating the objection—Question 15:

"How much of this decision is up to you?"

Isolating the objection—Question 16:

"And what is your personal perspective on this?"

Isolating the objection—Question 17:

"Can you tell me a little more about that, please?"

Isolating the objection—Question 18:

"How does upper management fit into this?"

Isolating the objection—Question 19:

"If you decided to go with this, is the budget there?"

Isolating the objection—Question 20:

"How about you? What are your feelings on this?"

Isolating the objection—Question 21:

"And how much influence do *you* have?"

Isolating the objection—Question 22:

"You know, I keep hearing you say _____, but I keep feeling that you mean something else. What might that be?"

Isolating the objection—Question 23:

"What aren't you telling me?"

Isolating the objection—Question 24:

"How would this fit into your (budget, plans, initiatives) right now?"

Isolating the objection—Question 25:

"I think what you are telling me is _____. Is that correct?"

Isolating the objection—Question 26:

"Don't you mean 'when' it works out?"

Isolating the objection—Question 27:

"If you're/they're a go on this, when would you like to see it implemented?"

Isolating the objection—Question 28:

"I'm sorry, I'm not following you. Can you tell me exactly what you mean?"

Isolating the objection—Question 29:

"How urgent for you (your company) is this right now?"

Isolating the objection—Question 30:

"_____, from where you are sitting right now, do you think this is a smart thing to do?"

Layer:

"Oh, and why not?"

Isolating the objection—Question 31:

"What would you need to see added to this to make it worthwhile for you?"

Isolating the objection—Question 32:

"What can I do right now to help you get into this?"

Isolating the objection—Question 33:

"Level with me: What is really holding you back?"

Isolating the objection—Question 34:

"What is really standing in the way of us working together?"

Isolating the objection—Question 35:

"Is there anything that I can do about it?"

Isolating the objection—Question 36:

"What do you seriously think it is going to take for us to work together?"

Isolating the objection—Question 37:

"What else should I know?"

As you can see, there are many ways to get your prospect talking to you. There are many ways to get them to open up and reveal what it will take or why the deal won't happen. If you are not asking some of these questions, then you are simply letting your prospect put you off, and your pipeline is filling with prospects who likely are not going to buy from you. Take some time right now to adjust four or five of these questions to fit your personality, your product or service, and fit them to the specific objections or stalls that you get. Then use them when that situation comes up. Remember, the best way to prepare for success is to prepare for it. So start now.

HOW TO OVERCOME THE "WE TRIED IT BEFORE AND IT DIDN'T WORK" OBJECTION

Years ago, when I first learned to how close sales over the phone, my manager got all the sales reps in the conference room, drew a big circle on the board, and put a bull in the middle of it. He called this the closing circle. He then used an eraser to create several breaks in the circle, in effect creating openings for the bull to run out of. He explained to us that the "doors" in the circle were objections and stalls the bull would use to escape the closing circle, and that our job was to answer each objection and "close each door," thereby blocking every excuse or exit of the bull. Once the circle was completely closed and the bull could no longer escape the closing circle, he would have no other option than to buy.

While I recognize that this isn't a very sophisticated analogy and that some people may even think it crude and not representative of today's interactive and consultative selling approach, I'd like to point out its essential truth: prospects are often going to give you more than one reason not to buy, and it is your job to be prepared to answer each objection, question, or concern, close the circle, and repeatedly ask for the order.

The important part of the preceding paragraph is "repeatedly ask for the order." Many sales reps may make one or two attempts to overcome an objection and then give up. Once they do, the "bull" simply walks through one of the remaining open doors and gets away. Only top closers have the fortitude and scripted responses to close *all* the doors and get the prospect to buy. And that is where having a prepared book of effective scripts comes in. The following objection is a great example. Prospects have many "doors" to escape through, and the objection, "We tried this before and it didn't work," is one of them. Many sales reps struggle to overcome this objection, but if you are prepared for it, it is easy to close this door. The following shows how.

"We Tried It Before, and It Didn't Work"

We tried it before—Response 1:

> "I understand, but there is something you have got to keep in mind. Today, technology changes so fast that a solution that came out just a few months ago is seldom comparable to its updated version even this week. You probably see this with apps. Heck, even Facebook comes out with improvements every two weeks. Do you use Facebook?"

(If yes)

> "Then you know what I mean."

(If no)

> "Well, I am sure you know what I mean, though."

"But here's the point: comparing our cutting-edge solution to something that you tried six months ago—or worse, two years ago!—is like comparing a model T Ford to today's feature-rich automobiles. It simply isn't the same—and nor will your experience be the same.

"Let me point out just two things that we do differently today from what you may have been used to in the past...."

(Point out two or three features you know are perfect for your prospect, then)

"So here is what I recommend you do: let's get you started on this and you can see for yourself why we are the number one solution for this."

There you have it: another door in the circle closed! After you use this close, watch your prospect try to escape through another door, and then simply close that one as well. Soon, once all the doors in the closing circle are closed, you will be in the final paperwork, and you will have yourself another new client!

How to Handle "I'll Have to Speak with...."

There are a few objections that seem—at first glance—almost impossible to overcome. "I want to think about it," is one of them. But a close second has to be the "I'll have to speak with" someone else: a supervisor, regional manager, spouse, and so on. In this case, like the one before it, the prospect isn't objecting, per se, but they are not saying yes, either. In both cases, however, they are stalling the sale and if your experience is like many others, then you know that a stalled sale often doesn't close. So what to do?

First of all, I hope you anticipated this stall and even gained some insight and leverage for it by uncovering it during the qualifying stage. A simple question like, "And besides yourself, who else weighs in on the decision on something like this?" would be enough to expose who all is involved in the decision process. Once you do, you can use any of the layering questions I have listed earlier.

But if you have found this out and you still get this stall when you ask for the deal at the end of your presentation, then you don't want to say what 80 percent of your competition says when they get this, which is, "When should I check back with you?" Instead, you want to begin delving into this stall and gain more insight into whether it is something that will potentially kill the deal, or if you can learn enough about the other person, or decision process, to properly access if this has the potential to turn into a sale and what it might realistically take to do so.

So the key to this stall is to begin questioning your prospect to learn as much as you can about the other person's buying motives and their decision process. As you begin asking some of the following questions, you will find that the more information they have about the other person's (decision maker's) process, the more likely it is they are involved in the buying decision as well. The less they know, the less involved they generally are, and, unfortunately, the less likely it is they can influence them. Choose any of the following questions, and use as many of them as appropriate. As always, spend some time to customize them to fit your product or service and your personality.

"I'll Have to Speak with My Regional Manager"

I'm going to speak with—Question 1:

> "Based on what you know about them, what is their timeline for acquiring this?"

> Layer:

> "And what sort of timeline are they dealing with for putting something like this to work for you?"

> I'm going to speak with—Question 2:

> "Share with me a little bit about the process they will go through to make a decision on this...."

> I'm going to speak with—Question 3:

> "Are they looking specifically for something like this right now, or are they in the information-gathering stage?"

I'm going to speak with—Question 4:

"What do you think some of the questions are that they will have on this?"

I'm going to speak with—Question 5:

"Is this something they specially tasked you to find, or are you going to be bringing this to them on your own?"

I'm going to speak with—Question 6:

"What questions can you see them having on this?"

I'm going to speak with—Question 7:

"Based on what I have shown *you* so far, do you think this is something they will approve?"

I'm going to speak with—Question 8:

"What concerns can you see them having on this?"

I'm going to speak with—Question 9:

"Does he/she tend to make quick decisions on something like this?"

I'm going to speak with—Question 10:

"What would be the biggest reason they wouldn't move on something like this?"

I'm going to speak with—Question 11:

"What would be the biggest reason they would go for this?"

I'm going to speak with—Question 12:

"Is your regional manager [wife/supervisor] generally supportive of your recommendations?"

I'm going to speak with—Question 13:

"Who besides your supervisor would be weighing in on this decision?"

I'm going to speak with—Question 14:

"Would it be okay for me to speak with them directly to answer any questions?"

I'm going to speak with—Question 15:

"I know you are going to explain this to them, but I don't want you to do my job for me. I'd be happy to reach out to them directly if that would be all right with you?"

I'm going to speak with—Question 16:

"What would be the best way for me to help them come to a positive answer on this?"

I'm going to speak with—Question 17:

"What would you recommend is the best way I can help them see the value in this?"

I'm going to speak with—Question 18:

"Can we do a conference call right now with them to just see what their initial reaction to this is?"

I'm going to speak with—Question 19:

"Based on the other suggestions you've taken to them, what do you think their reaction to this will be?"

I'm going to speak with—Question 20:

"You like this solution, right? And I take it you'll be recommending it to them then?"

I'm going to speak with—Question 21:

"Since we both think this solution will work for you, how can you and I persuade them to agree to go with us on this?"

As you can see from these questions, just because your prospect says they need to speak with someone, it doesn't mean that you have to go away. Instead, by asking questions and delving into the buying and

the decision-making process, you will learn what it is going to take for
you to advance and close the sale.

HOW TO HANDLE THE REFERENCES STALL

How do you handle when a prospect asks you for a reference? Do you
dutifully provide them with a list of happy clients they can call? And,
if you do, how many of those prospects actually call those references?
More important, do those prospects who call references ever close?

In my experience, when a prospect asks for references, they drop
down to about a 25 percent chance of becoming a closed sale. It is not
that my references are bad (you will see a rebuttal you can use that will
address this)—in fact, the references I give are of raving fans who have
used me with great results both professionally and personally. But still,
over many years of experience, references do not help close the sale as
much as you might think.

The reason for this is that asking for references always means the
same thing: your prospect is not sold on your company, on you, or on
your solution. When they ask you for a reference, they have something
particular in mind that they want to know more about, and they suspect
that you (or your company) can't provide it. Because of this, asking
for a reference is just a way to stall you so they can continue to do
research on other companies to find the one that addresses their main
(and hidden) concern.

That is why more than half of prospects who ask for a reference
don't even call them! I am sure you have noticed that in your own sales
experience. So the way to handle the reference stall (which is what it
really is) is once again to isolate this stall and get your prospect to reveal
what their real concern (or objection) is. The way to do that is to use
one of the following scripts:

"Do You Have Any References I Could Call?"

Reference stall—Response 1:

> "Absolutely. As you can imagine, I have a folder filled with happy and
> satisfied clients. But_____, let me ask you: Do you think I would give
> you a bad reference?"

(Let them respond.)

"Of course not. I'm only going to give you clients who love us and are happy with what we do for them. So what that tells me is that there is something you are either not convinced will work for you yet or that you don't think this is quite the fit you are looking for. So while you have me on the phone, please, level with me—what is the real issue that is holding you back?"

Reference stall—Response 2:

"I'd be happy to provide you with a reference or two, and let me ask you: If after you speak with them you hear what you need to hear, are you going to move forward with us and put us to work for you?"

(If yes)

"Great! Then hang on just a moment and let me get a client on the phone, and I'll conference you in. After you're done with your conversation, we can get you signed up...."

Reference stall—Response 3:

"_____, when someone asks you for a reference for your company or service, have you ever found that some people never even call the references?"

(Let them respond.)

"And don't you get the feeling that there is just something that is holding them back and they just aren't quite sold on your company yet?"

(Let them respond.)

"Well, since you have me on the phone right now, why don't you tell me what is holding you back or what you're concerned with, and I'll see if I can answer it for you."

Reference stall—Response 4:

"I'd be happy to. Now _____, as you might imagine, I have all different kinds of clients using this, so do me a favor: let me know the things that are concerning you, and I will then match you up with the right reference who can address those issues for you."

As you can see, when someone asks you for a reference, the most important thing you can do is isolate this stall and get your prospect to reveal what their real concern is. Unless you find out what that is, not only will your prospect not call your reference, but they may never call you back again, either.

HOW TO HANDLE "MY SUPPLIER IS MY FRIEND"

I often get asked the question of how to handle the objection: "My supplier is my friend/brother/long-term relationship, and so on." While this is, at first glance, a seemingly difficult objection to overcome—and sometimes, if it is true, won't be overcome right away—there are ways to position yourself to earn some of the business either right away, or to be the preferred vendor they reach out to if they need to consider making a change in the future. The way to do this effectively is to be prepared with proven scripts. Let's consider them one at a time.

"My Supplier Is My Friend"

The way to first deal with this is to explore the relationship briefly and then to qualify for an opening. Use:

"I understand, and I also do business with people I consider friends as well. Tell me, how long have you been doing business with him/her/them?"

Layer:

"And who were you doing business with before them?"

Layer:

"When was the last time you did a comparison with another provider?"

(If never)

"Well then, it is always a good idea to at least get another opinion/quote of services just so you know that you are not only getting the best deal and service, but also so you will know who to reach out to should you need additional help. Could I at least do a no-cost/no-obligation comparison quote for you?"

If your prospect says yes, then there is an opportunity here, and you have uncovered it. If they say no, then simply use the following next-in-line script.

"Okay, no problem. One last question: Could I be the next-in-line person you reach out to in case you ever need to get another quote or service comparison?"

(If yes, take all their information and offer to send your contact info and brochure.)

"Just out of curiosity, what would have to happen for you to even consider reaching out to someone else?"

This technique, if used as described here, is highly effective at getting your prospect to open up and reveal any possible opportunity.

"My Supplier Is My Brother/Relative"

As before, your first job is to question and explore this objection. Use:

"Hey that's great. As you know, doing business with relatives can have its upside and downside. How has your experience been?"

(If great)

"That's good to hear. Just out of curiosity, how long have you been doing business with [him/her/them]?"

Layer:

"And who did you use before that?"

Layer:

"And what did you like about doing business with a nonrelative that you miss now?"

(Regardless of what they say, layer)

"Well then, it's a good idea to at least get another opinion/quote of services so you know that you are not only getting the best deal and service, but also so you will know who to reach out to should you need additional help. Could I at least do a no-cost/no-obligation comparison quote for you?"

If your prospect says yes, then there is an opportunity here and you have uncovered it. If they say no, then simply use the next-in-line script that follows.

> "Okay. No problem. One last question: Could I be the next-in-line person you reach out to in case you ever need to get another quote or service comparison?"

(If yes, take all their information and offer to send your contact info and brochure.)

> "Just out of curiosity, what would have to happen for you to even consider reaching out to someone else?"

"I've Been Doing Business with My Current Supplier for a Long Time...."

> "How long has that been?"

Layer:

> "And has it been that long since you have compared prices and services with another provider?"

Or

> "You know, a lot has changed in that time. It sounds like this would be a good time to at least get another opinion/quote of services just so you know that you are not only getting the best deal and service, but also so you will know who to reach out to should you need additional help.

> "Could I at least do a no-cost/no-obligation comparison quote for you?"

If your prospect says yes, then there is an opportunity here and you have uncovered it. If they say no, then simply use the next-in-line script here:

> "Okay, no problem. One more question: Could I be the next-in-line person you reach out to in case you ever need to get another quote or service comparison?"

(If yes, take all their information and offer to send your contact info and brochure.)

> "Just out of curiosity, what would have to happen for you to even consider reaching out to someone else?"

As you can see, the way to deal with this objection is to get your prospect talking to see if there is an opportunity there. If you use these scripts, you will be surprised at what you could uncover.

How to Overcome the "You Expect Me to Make a Decision Now?" and "I Need to Do More Research" Objections

One of my e-zine readers sent me two objections he is struggling with, and they are: "We need to do some research first," and "I don't make on-the-spot decisions," or the variation: "Do you expect me to make a decision now?" Two interesting objections and two that are easy to handle—if you are prepared for them in advanced with good scripts.

Let's start with the second objection of "Do you expect me to make a decision now?" This is an objection that never should have come up to begin with because it should have been discovered and dealt with during the initial prospecting call. As I wrote earlier, during the prospecting call, you need to qualify your prospect in six different qualifying areas, and one of those is time frame. Here are a couple of qualifying questions on the cold call that would have prevented this objection from ever coming up:

You Expect Me to Make a Decision Now?

Qualifying for time frame—Question 1:

> "If you like our solution when we go over the presentation next week, what would be your time frame for putting it to use for you?"

> Qualifying for time frame—Question 2:

> "And if you like what you see next week, is this something you could make a decision on at that time?"

Again, these kinds of qualifying questions are the ones you ask during the initial call so you don't get this objection during the close.

Another way to avoid this objection is to requalify your prospect before giving your closing presentation. I always recommend you requalify at the beginning of your demo so you aren't ambushed with objections like, "Do you expect me to make a decision now?" Here are a couple of questions to ask before you begin your demo.

Requalifying before your presentation—Question 1:

"And, _____, let me ask you: If, after we finish the demo today, you like what you see and can see how it can help you [repeat their buying motive], is this something that you'd be in a position to make a decision on today?"

Requalifying before your presentation—Question 2:

"And, _____, let's talk about your time frame for putting this solution to work for you. If you like what you see today, how soon would you want to put it to work for you?"

Again, by using any of these techniques, you can avoid the two preceding objections. But what if you still get these objections at the end? The key here is to then isolate the objection so you can see what is really holding your prospect back. The best way to do that is to ask questions and listen.

Dealing with this objection—Response 1:

"What is your timeline then?"

"Based on what we have gone over today, how does this sound to you right now?"

Dealing with this objection—Response 2:

"I can certainly appreciate that, but while you are thinking it over, consider this...."

And keep pitching one or two points you know they really like. Then:

"Does that make sense to you?"

And, if it does, then ask for the order again:

"So why don't we do this...."

Never take one no (or two or three or four, for that matter) as the ultimate answer, but instead be ready to pitch the benefits and continue asking for the order.

The other objection: "We need to do some research first," can and should also be prevented by qualifying for timeline during the initial call, but if it still comes up, then treat it like any other stall and try to get to the real objection that is hiding behind it. And, as always, use a few proven scripts to make this easy and ask questions that are designed to get your prospects to reveal what it is going to take to close the sale.

We Need to Do Some Research

We need research—Response 1:

"I totally understand. Just out of curiosity, what parts do you need to do research on?"

We need research—Response 2:

"Okay, when you say research, does that involve comparing this to other companies?"

(If yes)

"And what part of this are you comparing the most?"

We need research—Response 3:

"I help my clients do research all the time. In fact, because I have access to so many resources in this industry, I can usually get answers and solutions they can't. Tell me, what specifically are you interested in learning more about?"

We need research—Response 4:

"And, based on what you know about it now, if your research comes back positive, does this sound like a solution that would work for you?"

(If yes)

"Great! And what is your timeline for acting on this?"

(If you get a date)

"Terrific! Then let me help you do the research so you can put this exciting (profitable, proven, and so forth) solution to work for you today!"

We need research—Response 5:

"_____, I have given you only part of my presentation because I didn't want to overwhelm you. But apparently I've left out some points that you need to know more about. Tell me, what specifically do you want more information on?"

We need research—Response 6:

"From what you *do* know about this so far, can you see this as being a fit for you?"

(If yes)

"Great. Tell me what I can do to help you learn more about this so we can put it to work for you today."

As you can see, the more you get your prospect to talk, the more information you will have as to what the real hold-up is, and what you can do to overcome it. Use the preceding scripts to help prevent some of these objections from ever coming up to begin with, or to isolate the real objection and close in on the solution that will work for each prospect.

HOW TO OVERCOME THE "MARKET/INDUSTRY/ECONOMY IS BAD" OBJECTION

You hear it all the time: "I/we can't do anything now because the _____ [fill in the blank with market or economy, or company, or industry, time of year, or budget, and so on] is down."

The crazy thing is that sales reps actually buy into this objection! I guess if you are not prepared to overcome it with a good script, and you keep getting it day in and day out, you *are* susceptible to buying into it.

I have even begun hearing sales teams jump on the "Oh things are terrible, the world is coming to an end...." objection and actually agreeing with their prospects! As soon as a sales rep gets this objection, I have heard them pile on with, "Oh, I've been hearing that a lot and things are bad out there! Some of our clients have even closed down their offices and let people go. Oh, it's terrible!" They then add:

"Well, if things turn around, then definitely give us a call...."

Empowering, huh?

Remember: On every sales call somebody is going to be sold. The only question is: Are your prospects going to sell you on why they are not buying (from you), or are you going to sell them on why they need you more than ever right now?

Because your product or service can almost always save them money or time or energy or manpower, or produce more and better results that will mean more revenue or business to them, then let's face it: they can't afford *not* to listen or meet with you!

Here is the only script you need to overcome the "Everything is terrible" objection and earn the right to meet or do a demo with your prospect: the next time you get any variation of the, "I/we can't do anything now because the _____ [fill in the blank with market or economy, or company, or industry, or budget, or time of year, and so forth] is down," objection, you simply say the following.

Market/Industry Economy Is Bad

Market is down rebuttal—Response 1:

"Well, because of that reason, I'm sure it's more important than ever for you to (reduce costs, save money, get more results, and so on), and that is exactly why other companies are meeting with us to see how we can do just that for them. You will be happy we met, too. Here is what I recommend we do...."

Market is down rebuttal—Response 2:

"_____, that is exactly why we should go over this demo together. You will learn how to better deal with this (time of year, slowdown in the economy, and so forth), and if nothing else, you will see how we handle this, and you will gain another perspective on how/what you can be doing to save costs. What is a good time next week for you?"

You have to be prepared with a positive, upbeat message to overcome their negativity, and you have to believe in what you are selling—in your solution—enough to earn the right to meet or present to your prospect.

Use the preceding scripts or adapt them to fit your personality and your product or service. When you do, you will start closing your prospects rather than letting them close you.

How to Overcome the "My Relative Handles That for Me" Objection and the "I Have a Longstanding Relationship with My Vendor" Objection

I know we already went through some rebuttals to this objection, but because it is getting to be so common, I wanted to give you even more proven ways to handle it here. If you are in B-to-C sales (business to consumer), then you no doubt get the objection (or some variation of it).

"My relative handles that for me, and I wouldn't be interested in changing."

In B-to-B sales (business to business), this objection often manifests as, "We've been doing business with them for years, and we get the best (rates, service, and so on, and we wouldn't be interested in switching."

Other variations include:

"We have a rep who visits us each week and we don't want to do business over the phone."

Or

"I've known my rep for years and we have a great relationship, so I wouldn't be interested."

Or

"Our supplier is the boss's son [or father, sister, pastor, and so on] and we only do business with people we know."

The list can go on and on. The tricky thing about this objection is that we can all relate to having a personal relationship with a family member or someone we really like and trust, so we feel awkward trying to overcome it. Here is the thing: sometimes this is a real objection, but sometimes it is just a smokescreen that works on salespeople, so the prospect keeps using it. Either way, here are some additional ways to get around it, or, at least, to set the prospect up so they are thinking about you when that relationship changes.

I Have a Longstanding Relationship

Existing relationship close—Response 1:

"I totally know how that is, and I'm not here to come between you and that relationship. But hey, everything changes, as you know, and if something should change between how you are doing things now, it's always good to have done your research in advance so you are not scrambling later.

"Why don't we at least get together briefly, and I will give you some solid options in case you ever need them. . . ."

Existing relationship close—Response 2:

"I understand and you know, _____, every now and then initiatives change. Sometimes you might need a lower price, or more variety of product, or who knows. The point is that it's always good to know what else is out there.

"How about this: It doesn't cost anything to at least compare what else is out there these days, and who knows, if things change with you, at least you will know who to call to ask questions. Let's do this. . . ."

Existing relationship close—Response 3:

"Glad your [brother-in-law, sister-in-law, and so on] is handling this for you, but heaven forbid anything ever happen, you know a divorce or a falling out, you will be happy you've got a good back-up! Let's do this. . . ."

(Then set an appointment.)

Existing relationship close—Response 4:

"Well, _____, you know how life is—people can get sick, or change jobs, or whatever—the smart thing for you to do is to always have a back-up ready, you know, just in case."

"Since it doesn't cost anything to learn about our services and prices, why don't I drop by?"

Existing relationship close—Response 5:

"Because things have changed a lot since you've been working with (him/her), I suggest you at least be prudent and learn about what the current market has to offer you. Who knows? You may find that there is an even easier/less expensive option available to you and you can let them know about it! Let's do this. . . ."

Existing relationship close—Response 6:

"I'm happy you have found someone you've been able to trust for all these years. Let me ask you this: If something changes with that relationship and you find that you need to look elsewhere, could I be the next-in-line person you speak to about getting this (product/service) from?"

(If yes, get their information and give yours, then)

"_____, just out of curiosity, what might have to happen for you to even begin looking?"

Now you have even more ways to handle what may have seemed like an almost impossible objection in the past. Will all of these always work? No. Will some of them work a lot better than what you are probably saying now? Absolutely!

CHAPTER **9**

Winning Closing Techniques

I n addition to the word-for-word scripts to the specific objections provided earlier, there are other strategies and techniques that every top producer knows and uses almost intuitively. By learning the following six proven techniques, and weaving them into your closing presentations, you will gain confidence and more control over the selling process. You will also avoid the routine problems other sales reps create, and you will learn even more ways of getting buy-in throughout your presentation and of persevering to win the sale. As always, don't just read the following techniques, study them, and work to incorporate them into your closing repertoire of skills. The more skillful you get, the easier closing will become, and the more sales and money you will make.

HOW TO USE TIE-DOWNS TO BUILD MOMENTUM

I don't know why tie-downs aren't used more by sales reps selling over the phone. They serve several crucial functions, one of which is getting confirmation that the point you just made was understood and accepted by your prospect. This is especially important when selling over the phone, as you don't have the visual clues that tell you how your pitch is going. Using tie-downs frequently, however, give you this information and also give you the confidence to move on to the next part of your pitch.

Using tie-downs is also instrumental in building that all-important "yes momentum." If the prospect keeps agreeing with you, then you can feel confident at the end of your pitch in asking for the sale. This eliminates the drama and uncertainty that often accompanies the end of a presentation. Wouldn't you want to know in advance the likely direction a prospect will go when you finally ask for the sale? Tie-downs scattered throughout your presentation will give you this crucial insight.

Tie-downs also give your prospect a chance to engage with you, because when you use one you actually have to wait for them to respond. Listening to what a prospect responds with—and how (tone, inflection, pacing) he/she responds—gives you important feedback as to how your presentation is going. Often, if you hear hesitation or boredom or disbelief in your prospect's voice, you can stop your presentation and address it. Doing this keeps you and your prospect in sync and makes it much easier for you to confidently ask for the sale at the end.

Using tie-downs also gives you control over the flow of the call. I cannot tell you how many sales reps I listen to who get manhandled by prospects who immediately take control of the call by firing questions at them. The sales rep becomes passive, and after the prospect gets all the answers he or she needs, they move to end the call and think about it. This gives all sales reps a sick feeling, and many reps feel used after a call goes this way. It is easy to turn this around—just finish your answer by asking a question of your prospect. Remember, whoever asks a question is in control of the call.

There are many other valuable reasons for using tie-downs, but let us look at some of the most effective ones now and go over the situations in which they work the best:

Situation 1: Whenever your prospect asks you a buying question (and any question a prospect asks you is a buying question), and you answer it, you must use a tie-down. For example, if a prospect asks you how much something costs, after you give them the price, you absolutely must use a tie-down. Any of these work well.

Buying Question Tie-Down

Price tie-down 1:

"How does that price sound?"

Price tie-down 2:

"Is that what you were looking to spend today?"

Price tie-down 3:

"How does that compare with what you are paying now?"

Price tie-down 4:

"Is that within your budget?"

Price tie-down 5:

"That is a great value today, and I would take as many as I could at that price—how many should I ship you today?"

(Okay, that's a close, but I couldn't help myself! Do you see how tie-downs can lead to a close?)

If a prospect asks a question about a feature or a benefit, use any of the following.

Benefit Question Tie-Down

After delivering a benefit tie-down 1:

"Do you see how that works?"

After delivering a benefit tie-down 2:

"What do you think of that?"

Layer:

"Oh?"

(Then hit mute and force them to elaborate.)

After delivering a benefit tie-down 3:

"How would you use that?"

After delivering a benefit tie-down 4:

"Do you understand how that would help in your environment?"

After delivering a benefit tie-down 5:

"I think that is a great benefit—how about you?"

If a prospect makes a statement that seems negative, use the following.

Negative Statement Tie-Down

Negative follow-up tie-down 1:

"How did you come to that?"

Negative follow-up tie-down 2:

"Compared to what?"

Negative follow-up tie-down 3:

"What do you mean exactly?"

Negative follow-up tie-down 4:

"How does your current vendor handle that?"

Situation 2: Use tie-downs *throughout* your presentation. Most sales reps power through their presentations and use far too few tie-downs or check-ins. If they do use them, they are usually closed-ended, which leads their prospect to reveal little. Use these more open-ended tie-downs to engage *and* learn crucial buying motives.

Presentation Tie-Downs

Tie-downs during your presentation 1:

"That is how we drive the leads. Now, tell me about how you would get the most out of this."

Tie-downs during your presentation 2:

"That is one of our biggest selling points. Tell me: How would this affect how you are currently doing things?"

Tie-downs during your presentation 3:

"Do you see how this works?"

Layer:

"How might this affect you?"

Tie-downs during your presentation 4:

"Are you with me there?"

Layer:

"What questions do you have?"

Tie-downs during your presentation 5:

"That is a nice feature, don't you think?"

Layer:

"How would that work for you?"

Tie-downs during your presentation 6:

"Is this sounding like it might work for you?"

(Okay, there I go again! Do you see how after a few tie-downs, it is just natural for you to start using trial closes?)

Tie-downs during your presentation 7:

"What do you think of this so far?"

Tie-downs during your presentation 8:

"Would this work at your location?"

Layer:

"How many other locations would this work for?"

Tie-downs during your presentation 9:

"How many other departments would want one of these as well?"

Tie-downs during your presentation 10:

"That is pretty special, isn't it?"

Tie-downs during your presentation 11:

"Do you see why this is so popular?"

Tie-downs during your presentation 12:

"Tell me, would that fit into your budget?"

Tie-downs during your presentation 13:

"Most people like this. How does it sound to you?"

Tie-downs during your presentation 14:

"Will that work for you?"

Layer:

"Tell me how...."

Tie-downs during your presentation 15:

"What else do you need to know?"

Tie-downs during your presentation 16:

"What other area are you interested in?"

Tie-downs during your presentation 17:

"Would that be a deal killer for you?"

Layer:

"And what would be the workaround for that?"

Tie-downs during your presentation 18:

"Would that be enough for you to move forward with this?"

Tie-downs during your presentation 19:

"Tell me: How close are you to wanting to move forward with this?"

(There I go again!)

Let me reiterate that using tie-downs gives you the nonverbal information you don't have because you can't see your prospect's reaction (because you are selling over the phone). Therefore, it is critical for you to begin using more of the preceding tie-downs during every conversation. Remember, the more you can get your prospect talking, the more you will learn what it will take to close the sale.

TOO MANY OPTIONS? NARROW IT DOWN TO GET THE SALE NOW

If you sell a product or service with many add-ons and options or choices, then it is easy for your prospect to get overwhelmed and want to think about it. Many sales reps actually make it harder for buyers to decide because they keep pitching (instead of closing) and so complicate the sale even further. This is called talking past the close, and besides stalling or delaying making a decision, it can also lead to introducing new objections. This is not what you ever want to do.

You want instead to simplify the sale and make it easy for your prospect or customer to buy something now, rather than putting the decision off. Here are some ways you can do that. As always, take some time to customize these to fit your product or service.

Narrow It Down

Narrow the options down 1:

> "Now I may have made this harder on you than I should have. Let's look at the basic package again, the [restate the easiest offer], and let me ask you: Will this do most of the things you are looking at this to do for you?"

Narrow the options down 2:

> "It is easy to get overwhelmed by all the choices and combinations, so let me make this easy for you: most people in your position go for our basic package because they find it does everything they need it to do. And, of course, you can always upgrade later should you have the need.
>
> "So let's do this. . . ."

Narrow the options down 3:

> "I'm getting the feeling we've gone over too many options, and it would probably be easier for you if we just took half of these away. Which features don't you feel you need?"

Narrow the options down 4:

"I know it is easy to go back and forth on some of these combinations, so let me ask you: Is this a toss-up decision, or are you leaning toward one more than the other—and if so, which one is it?"

Narrow the options down 5:

"_____, let's step back here for a moment. You don't have to get the package that has all the bells and whistles, unless you really want to, of course. So tell me, which one of these are you leaning toward?"

Narrow the options down 6:

"You know, going through all the possible options and combinations could take you hours and hours. You don't have to do that now. Instead, let's break this down to your absolute must-haves: Which features can't you live without?"

Narrow the options down 7:

"If you had to pick one package or combination over another, which would it be?"

Narrow the options down 8:

"With all of these options you are going to get our (warranty, performance, delivery, and so forth), so any package you pick is going to work well for you. Tell me, what are you leaning toward right now?"

Narrow the options down 9:

"_____, let's make this simple and get you started with the basic package for now. That way you can see how this works for you, we can get into a relationship, and later, down the road, if you want to expand your coverage, you can. At least in the meantime you are not missing out on these results."

Narrow the options down 10:

"Let's do this: let's take the premium package so you won't have to worry later that you are missing out on something you wish you had gotten in the beginning. With this package, you will get everything you need."

Having these closes handy when you feel your prospect slipping away, or is having a hard time making a decision, could very well save the sale for you.

Boost Your Sales by Using This One Word

Catchy title, huh? "Boost your sales using just this *one* word." Wouldn't it be nice if there *was* just one magic word that could really increase your sales?

There is!

Before I tell you what it is, though, let me give you a brief background on how I discovered it. Years ago, when I was struggling to make sales, I found a bad pattern had developed in regard to how my sales attempts were ending up. After pitching and pitching, most of my sales were being stalled with some variation of:

"Let me think about it."

Or

"I'll have to discuss this with my partner...."

Or

"Okay, why don't you get back to me in a few weeks?"

Sound familiar? It should. Many sales presentations end this way. After racking my brain for the reason, I finally began listening to how the top closers in my company were closing their sales, and, more important, how they were opening and qualifying their prospects as well.

It turns out they were all using one magic word.

The word was "today."

And that is when I started using it as well, and it didn't just boost my sales, it catapulted them! In fact, it even had much more impact than that. It also greatly reduced the number of unqualified leads I sent out and spent hours of useless time with.

Here are some examples of how to use this powerful word "today" in both your opening and closing statements.

For Qualifying

You must qualify each prospect's timeline and set the proper expectation for the close. At the end of your prospecting or cold call, and before you schedule your demo or send your information, you must ask something like these.

While Prospecting

"Today" examples while prospecting 1:

> "So, _____, I have got you on the calendar to do a walk-through of our solution next Wednesday, and if after we're done, you really like this, is it something that you can make a decision on at that time?"

> "Today" examples while prospecting 2:

> "So, _____, I look forward to our demo next Wednesday, and if after we are done, you really like this, I'm going to ask you for a simple yes or no. Is that fair?"

In some situations, if you are dealing with an influencer, your question will be more about what the next steps are, what the decision maker's time frame is, how many other companies they are looking at, and so on. But if you are dealing with the owner or decision maker, you must get a firm commitment as to time frame so you can confirm a decision right after your pitch.

For Closing Calls

At the beginning of your presentation, before you go into your slide show or however you do it, you requalify by asking the following.

While Closing

"Today" examples while closing 1:

> "I am excited to show you this, and at the end, if you feel this is the right solution for you, this is something you can move on *today*, right?"

That's it. No wishy-washy way around it. You must set a clear expectation right from the beginning (and that means on the qualifying call) and then reconfirm it at the beginning of the close. If you have set this up on your prospecting call, then you can open this way:

"Today" examples while closing 2:

"_____, as discussed last week, I will go over everything about how this works for you, and answer any of your questions. At the end I'm going to ask you for a simple yes or no decision on this today. Okay?"

I know what you're thinking: "What if they say no?" Then you adjust your presentation to target their buying motives and start overcoming what their objection or stall is. I have written many effective scripts to help you do that, and if you want more, get a copy of my bestselling book *The Ultimate Book of Phone Scripts* here: http://mrinsidesales.com/ultimatescripts.htm.

Bottom line: you will make more sales faster and with less effort *if* you set the proper expectation on the front call and confirm it by opening your closing call using the magic word: "today."

Try it *today* and see for yourself.

TEN WAYS TO SOFTEN THE PRICE OBJECTION AND KEEP PITCHING

Many sales reps get thrown off their pitch when a prospect objects to something early on during the close. For example, when talking about the price of a product or service, if the prospect interrupts and says something like, "Oh, that's way too much," many sales reps don't know how to respond. Because they are not prepared with a good script, they default to ad-libbing and this often leads them to say the wrong thing. The wrong thing in this case is to stop and try to overcome the objection.

Instead, it is often wiser to retain control of the call by acknowledging the objection and then continuing with your presentation. Doing so not only keeps you in control of the direction of the call, but it also allows you the chance to build more value. We have already gone over the various times you can handle objections, and here are some additional ways to postpone dealing with a concern or objection and continuing with your presentation.

If a price or price range is given (say, anywhere from \$5,000 to \$25,000), and the prospect objects with, "That's more than we want to spend," then instead of stopping and trying to overcome the objection (which only gives control to the prospect and disrupts your momentum), you should respond with any of the following.

Soften the Price

Soften the price and keep pitching 1:

> "That is only a range, and I will explain how that works in just a moment...."

Then continue on with your pitch.

Soften the price and keep pitching 2:

> "There are some other options, but first let me explain how this works and how it can affect you (or your company or other departments, and so on)."

Then continue on with your pitch.

Soften the price and keep pitching 3:

> "Based on what you know now, it may seem like a lot, but let me get through exactly what you get for this...."

Then continue on with your pitch.

Soften the price and keep pitching 4:

> "_____, you obviously don't have to go with this at all, and I am not asking you to make a decision right now. Instead, let me finish explaining how this works, what you get, and how it might work for you [or your company, and so on].

> "After that, you will be in a better position to decide what to do next. Fair enough?"

Soften the price and keep pitching 5:

> "Let's put the budget aside for a moment and first see if this is a solution that would even work for you. What I will do is explain everything to you,

answer your questions, and then we can address whether it provides the value to justify the investment, okay?"

Soften the price and keep pitching 6:

"The value this provides is quite worth the investment—as you will see. Let me finish explaining how this works and what my other clients are getting out of it. Then you can decide what—if anything—you want to do. Now...."

Continue on with your pitch.

Soften the price and keep pitching 7:

"Let's put budget aside for a moment and let me show you how this can positively affect what you are spending now...."

Back to your pitch.

Soften the price and keep pitching 8:

"I know at this point it might seem like a lot, but I guarantee once you understand the whole picture, you will easily see the value here...."

Back to your pitch.

Soften the price and keep pitching 9:

"_____, those are only the price ranges, and what you decide to ultimately spend will be entirely your decision and based only on whether you see enough benefit to move forward. Let me show you...."

Back to your pitch.

Soften the price and keep pitching 10:

"_____, until we qualify your business, we won't know what your payment options are, so let's not get ahead of ourselves. What I recommend is we go through the approval process and then you can decide if this is worth it for you or not. Fair enough?"

Remember, the point here is not to get thrown off early in your pitch just because a prospect objects to the price. Instead, you want to maintain control, build value, and get buy-in during your presentation. You can do that by using any of the preceding rebuttals to soften the price objection.

IN SALES, THE MOST IMPORTANT THING TO SAY IS. . . .

I know, it's catchy, and kind of a trick title, isn't it? When I ask audiences what they think it is, they guess things like:

"Asking for the sale!"

"When would the customer like delivery?"

"How many units do they want?"

Things like that. All these are good guesses—they are all closing questions and these are arguably the most important things to say. But the number one most important thing to say is. . . . nothing.

That's right. Remaining silent after asking a qualifying question, or a tie-down, or a trial close, or especially after asking for the sale, is the most important thing to do. Another crucial time to say nothing is after a prospect gives an objection. This is important because if you can just give some space here before you respond, you will find that your prospect will often feel compelled to explain their reasoning or even reveal what you will need to say to overcome it. And so saying nothing during these moments is actually your most powerful tool.

The reason for this is that your prospect or customer has all the answers as to why they will buy or not buy, and if you don't remain quiet and let them tell you, you will never know what they are. The problem for 90-plus percent of salespeople is that they want to talk instead of suffer through what they interpret as an uncomfortable silence. But it is just this silence that will *always* encourage your prospect to reveal more, and the more they reveal, the more insight and leverage you will have to close the sale.

So how can you get good at *not* saying anything? Simple: use your mute button. For most reps, the mute button is something they seldom use (do you even know where yours is?), and if they do occasionally use it, it is to put a prospect on hold to get some information or look something up. But for top sales producers, the mute button is *the most* powerful button on their phone. Here's how to use it:

- First, locate it, start practicing using it—you know, get comfortable with the time delay (if any) between when you turn it on and turn it off. Reassure yourself that there is no clicking noise and that it is absolutely seamless.

- Know when to use it. This is simple, actually. Whenever you ask a question of a prospect, hit your mute button. *Do not* unmute yourself until your prospect is done with their thought and done speaking.

- In fact, put a two- or three-second delay between when you think they are done and when you unmute. This is harder than it seems, but will pay dividends.

- *Special Tip Here:* Contrary to what you think, your prospect does not need to hear your um's or ah's to believe you are listening. The more absolute quiet there is, the more comfortable they will feel, and the more they will talk.

- Get in the habit of encouraging them to talk even more by unmuting yourself (after they are done) and asking, "Oh?" or "What else?" or "What do you mean exactly?" Then mute yourself again and let them continue talking.

- Take notes while they talk. Write down any words or phrases they say and make it a point to feed these back to them later in the conversation. This will show them you are actively listening, and they will be more receptive to common words and phrases they use often.

- The mute button is good for prospecting calls as well! Do not just use it during the close. In fact, your tip is that whenever your prospect is talking, you need to be on mute.

The treasure of information you will get by listening and not interrupting is beyond valuable.

Not only will you get the exact reasons and motives needed to close the sale (or objections to avoid or overcome), but you will get something else just as valuable: you will gain trust and confidence.

Everyone loves to be heard and loves to be listened to. Most sales-people are distrusted and disliked because they are pushy and make it seem as if it is all about them. You can immediately reverse this by becoming a great listener.

Quick Last Story: just the other day I was speaking with a new prospect and, employing the mute button, the call went for an hour and 40 minutes. The prospect probably talked for an hour and 15 minutes of that time. When the call finally ended, he told me how much he enjoyed the conversation and how much he was looking forward to the next call. And all I did was ask pointed questions and then listened while on mute. So there you have it: the most important thing to say in sales is.... nothing!

ASK FOR THE SALE FIVE TIMES—AT LEAST!

How many times have you seen a commercial (either a TV ad, a public billboard, an ad in a magazine, and so on) for Coca-Cola? Perhaps I should ask how many times a *day* do you see one? You think that people already know about Coca-Cola, but did you know that Coca-Cola still spends millions of dollars each year on advertisements? Why do you think that is?

It is the same reason that infomercials run over and over again. After you have seen the same infomercial 50 times, you begin to consider it. After another 50 times, you think you might use it. Another 50, and some of you decide that you've got to have it. I mean, heck, they have run this commercial at least a thousand times. There must be some value to this, right?

I remember my first sales manager used to say to us that we weren't even in the closing arena until we had asked for the sale at least five times (and gotten a "no" five times, by the way).

After that, he would say, you are finally closing. I would attempt to argue with him, saying that if I kept asking, then I would become a pest. He pointed out that when a prospect objects to something, it was my job as a sales professional to handle the objection using a scripted response, then confirm my answer, and then ask for the sale again. He told me this is what "closing the sale" was called.

How many times do you ask for the sale? Do you ask for it in a round-about, soft way and then give up if your prospect says no? Or do you even ask for it at all? How much more successful would you be if you asked for the order five times and had a prepared response to each objection and, after answering it, asked for the sale again? Now I know there is a fine line between being obnoxious and being persistent, but the more you can be persuasive and persistent, the more deals you are going to close. It is like Coca-Cola. If they had run one ad and quit, we would all be drinking Pepsi today!

So, what is the best way to ask for the order over and over again? You have options: you can use trial closes, assumptive closes, or flat out closes. Here are some scripts to get you started.

Ask for the Sale

Closing statements 1:

> "Have I given you enough to say yes yet, or do you need to hear more?" (Soft trial close)

Closing statements 2:

> "Do you have any more questions or have you decided to put us to work for you?" (Soft trial close)

Closing statements 3:

> "Most people choose the starter pack and that works out great for them. Would you like that, or do you think the professional package is better for you?" (Alternative close)

Closing statements 4:

> "Our system can be set up in a matter of a week—and the sooner you give us the okay, the sooner it will be working for you. Would you like to get started with this today?" (Close)

Closing statements 5:

> "That is how my other client got over that hurdle. I would recommend you do the same. You will always be glad you did. Let's go ahead and get you signed up for this. Which credit card would you like to use today?" (Close after overcoming an objection)

Closing statements 6:

"Since your (partner, wife, spouse, and so on) goes with whatever you think is best, they will probably go with this as well. In the meantime, let's go ahead and get the paperwork done and a delivery date set. If they change your mind, you can simply call back in, but in the meantime, you will have this all completed. Now how would you like to pay for this?" (Overcoming the partner objection close)

Closing statements 7:

"Now _____, we can go back and forth on this, and I'm sure you can come up with many more reasons not to do this. But let's face it: you know you need it, and I know you want it! So let's go ahead and move forward. What is your preferred payment method today?" (Flat out close)

Closing statements 8:

"It sounds like you understand this now, so let's get you started. What address do you want this delivered to?" (Assumptive close)

Closing statements 9:

"Did I answer that for you? Do you have any more questions? No? Okay, great—then welcome aboard! I know you are going to enjoy this as much as my other clients do. How would you like to pay for this today?" (Close)

Closing statements 10:

"As my dad used to say, 'There's nothing to it but to do it!' So let's do this today. Where do you want us to send this to today?"

If you have done your job up front and properly qualified your prospect, chances are they actually want to buy from you. So make it easy on them by asking for the sales at least five times. Remember, the magic happens around the seventh close.

CHAPTER 10

Follow-Up Strategies

Now we get to the part of the sale that top producers really excel in: planning for and following through up with prospects that don't close right away. Believe it or not, many sales reps make half-hearted attempts to pursue a prospect who puts them off, and when they do follow up, if they are put off again, they often give up or let themselves be defeated by voice mail or emails that go unreturned. As you'll learn in this chapter, effective follow strategies are a key to the success of top producers. They recognize follow ups as just another recurring selling situation, and because of this they prepare in advance with best practice techniques that help them succeed. And after reading and following the techniques and proven strategies in this chapter, you will too!

THE PROPER WAY TO SET A CALL BACK

Not all sales close on the first—or even second or third, and so on—closing call. Because of that, it is often necessary to set a call back to move the sale forward. Like most parts of a sale, the call back is one of those recurring selling situations that you, or your sales team, will find yourself in countless times a day or week. Because of this, it is important that you develop and then script out a best-practice approach to handle it effectively. Unfortunately, many sales reps have never given the call back (or very many other parts of their sale) much thought. Instead, they ad-lib it and so develop ineffective and bad habits. Some of these include:

"Ah, when should I follow up with you?"

This is obviously a weak set-up and gives all control of the call—and the ensuing sales cycle—over to the prospect. As strange as it may sound, this is how over 50 percent of sales reps handle the call back. Another ineffective approach is:

> "When will you be speaking with _____? Okay, would it be all right if I followed up after that?"

Again, this is a weak approach and gives all control to the prospect. While there are some instances when you need to find out what the next step is, (that is, talking to a partner, meeting with a committee, and so forth), what is important is that you, the sales rep, take control of the call back time frame and get a commitment from your prospect. Here are some examples of the proper way to set a call back.

Proper Way

Setting a call back 1:

> "_____, in terms of talking to your partner, what time today can you do that?"

Why not shorten the callback period by assuming they will be speaking with the other person that same day? This works best in a small company or in a business-to-consumer sale. Trying this close first is always your best option, and you will be surprised by how many of your prospects will be ready to speak with you later that same day.

If you know it is going to be later in the week or another time, then change the script accordingly.

Setting a callback 2:

> "_____, when is the soonest you will be speaking with them?"

After they let you know, say the following.

Setting a call back 3:

> "Okay, great. I am looking at my calendar for that day. What is better for you on that Tuesday, morning or afternoon?"

Now you are locking down not only the day, but also the time. You are getting them involved and having them check their schedule. Once again, *you* are controlling the call back, and by doing it this way you are not letting a lot of time pass between when they speak to their partner and when you next speak again. If there are a lot of decision makers involved, or if it is going to be a longer process, then you should schedule a "progress call" to access their level of interest and to keep yourself in the loop.

Setting a call back 4:

"I understand there are several people involved in this and that you are talking to other vendors. Here is what I suggest: since you are likely to have some questions come up between our next call, how about I reach out to you in (one week or two weeks, whatever is appropriate) just to see if there is anything I can answer for you.

"I've got my calendar in front of me. How does [suggest a day and time] look for you?"

Once again, you are driving the sales cycle and the call back. This is crucial to keep you top of mind and to allow you to head off any problems that might come up during the decision process.

Setting a call back 5:

"I will go ahead and send you the information we just talked about, and then I'll schedule you in for a call back next Tuesday. Do you have your calendar handy?"

Noticing a trend? Once again, *I am* in control of the call back time frame. And don't worry—if that is not okay with your prospect, they will suggest another day and time that is. Setting a call back like this keeps the sale moving forward, and keeps them from falling through the cracks.

Now what happens if *they* want to call you back and won't allow you to set the call back? Two things: one is that this isn't a good sign. It means they want to control the sales cycle (which is never good), and, number two, it can also mean there is an objection that is standing in the way of the sale. When this happens, you should try to move the call back date out just a little further and still try to control when you get to call back.

Setting a call back 6:

"I understand. What is the timeline for this?"

Qualify for the timeline first. Then:

Setting a call back 7:

"Tell you what: if I don't hear from you in the next (30 days or whatever is appropriate), then I will reach back out to you to see if there are any questions. What do you prefer, mornings or afternoons?"

Once again, *you* are in control of the call back, and you now have a definite time frame and time of day to call back. The bottom line with the call back call is to keep control of when it happens. Never leave it up to your prospect. Try to lock down the soonest date after any event that is going to happen, like them speaking to a partner, and so forth. Next, get them involved by having them check their calendar and identify a time of day. Try to get their buy-in on that day.

By getting better at controlling the sales cycle, you will get closer to making deals happen. Make it a point to get good at this—and all other parts of the sale. As you do, your sales will become easier, and you will soon have the confidence—and the income—of the top producers in your company or industry!

HOW TO FOLLOW UP WITH PROSPECTS AND WIN BUSINESS

A while ago, my wife and I renovated our new home, and as part of this grueling process, we had to get many quotes from all different kinds of people. This ranged from window replacement people, plumbers, electrical contractors, painters, tile companies, contractors, fine craftsman, window treatment companies—the list seemed endless. After they finally showed up and saw the work, their next job was to deliver a quote (usually by email). As a sales trainer, the next part seemed pretty straightforward to me—and that was for them to follow up on their quotes, right?

Would you believe that over 90 percent of these people *never* followed up on their quote? I am absolutely amazed by that! It makes me understand and believe even more in a card that I send to many of my potential clients:

Sales Statistics

48 percent of salespeople never follow up with a prospect

25 percent of salespeople make a second contact and stop

12 percent of salespeople make only three contacts and stop

Only 10 percent of salespeople make more than three contacts

2 percent of sales are made on the first contact

3 percent of sales are made on the second contact

5 percent of sales are made on the third contact

10 percent of sales are made on the fourth contact

80 percent of sales are made on the fifth to twelfth contact

Interesting statistics, aren't they? I always follow up with prospects—and many, many times as well—and that practice alone has made me more successful than most of my competition. And after my recent experience with these contractors, I am even more convinced that just following up regularly gives you a significant edge over your competition. Here is a sample follow-up campaign (emails and phone calls) I use that you can adapt to your sales cycle as well.

Follow-Up Emails

After my initial phone call with a prospect—whether they want information or links to my website, or just want to talk it over—I always send a separate email thanking them for taking the time to speak with me.

Email 1:

Dear [prospect's name]:

Thank you for taking a few minutes today to tell me a little about your company and what you are trying to accomplish. It sounds like if I can help you [repeat their specific needs here], then there might be a fit between our companies.

I have sent over the [proposal, specs, job scope, whatever you promised] as well as a meeting request and look forward to our next conversation on [confirm the time for your next contact]. If you have any questions before we speak, please don't hesitate to call me back on my direct dial phone number: [your number].

Once again, thank you for taking the time to speak with me, and I look forward to continuing our conversation next week.

Sincerely,

[your signature and company info]

Email 2:

My next contact comes two days later. It always includes something that might be of interest to my prospect. Here is a sample email:

Dear [prospect's name]:

I was thinking about you and thought you would enjoy seeing/reading the following article: [name of an article, company brochure, white paper, something related to their needs]. I think this aligns with what you are trying to accomplish.

Let me know if there is anything else I can do to help you. Once again, my direct phone number is: [your number].

Looking forward to speaking with you next [day and time of appointment].

Sincerely,

[your signature and company info]

Follow-Up Calls

Opening call back:

My next contact comes with a phone call on the date we have scheduled to speak next. (You *did* get a specific day and time for your next contact, right?) Often, before this point, I will also send out an automatic meeting reminder as well. My opening for this call is very assumptive and avoids common mistakes such as: "I'm just calling to follow up," or "I'm just calling to see if you had time to read the material I sent you," or "Did you have time to go through our website?" and so on. Instead your opening call should something like:

"Hi, _____, this is _____ with [your company], how's your Monday going? You know, _____, I've been looking forward to speaking with you today. I'm sure you looked over the information I sent and probably have some questions, so tell me, where would you like to start?"

Again, always be assumptive, and obviously vary your opening based on whether you are doing a demo (a requalify in this case), or simply assume they have done what they committed to doing and then ask a question to get them to reveal what they are thinking.

So, by now—by this second conversation—I have been in contact with my prospect four times. The first was our initial conversation.

The second was the email, "Thanks for taking the time." The third was the meeting request. The fourth is the next email with additional information or an article. Including this follow-up call, I have now reached out to my prospect five times! But this is just the start.

After my presentation, I get a specific day and time to follow up again, and I will send another email article or white paper in between this. And if my prospect is not available when I call back, I call them several times a day during the week until we connect—and, of course, I also send emails.

In addition to this, any prospect in my pipeline also goes into my Send Out Cards campaign, from which they get a physical greeting card from me in the mail each month until they buy. (More about this system in the next section.) If you want to peek at this amazing card system, you can look at it here: www.sendoutcards.com/mrinsidesales.

On average, between emails and phone conversations and meeting reminders, my prospects get from six to eight contacts within the first two or three weeks. Then they get a card in the mail each month as well.

And last, if a prospect goes dark during or after this, I always send them my "Should I Stay or Should I Go" email, which gets me a response over 65 percent of the time—even when every other method fails to get them to react. This is such a powerful tool that I will list it here for you again.

Subject Line: [prospect name] Should I Stay or Should I Go?

Dear _____:

I haven't heard back from you, and that tells me one of three things:

1. You've filled the position or you've already chosen another company for this.

2. You're still interested but haven't had the time to get back to me yet.

3. You've fallen and can't get up, and in that case please let me know and I'll call 911 for you.

Please let me know which one it is because I'm starting to worry.

Honestly, all kidding aside, I understand you are really busy, and the last thing I want to do is be pain in the neck once a week. Whether your schedule has just been too demanding or you've gone another direction,

I would appreciate it if you would take a second to let me know so I can follow up accordingly.

Thank you in advance, and I look forward to hearing back from you.

Kind regards,

If this email made you laugh, then think about getting your prospects to laugh as well. Again, this email gets over 65 percent of my prospects to email me back to let me know their status. Try it; it works!

As you can see, having a follow-up system—and sticking to it—will put you ahead of more than 90 percent of your competition. And if you have qualified a lead properly in the beginning, then this kind of perseverance is often enough to win you the business most of the time.

STAYING TOP OF MIND ACROSS A LONGER TIME FRAME

As you have no doubt experienced, and despite your best efforts, sometimes a prospect doesn't buy for some reason. Oftentimes, circumstances have changed: they may have attempted to handle the situation internally, or initiatives have changed, or they may have decided to try another vendor or stick with their existing supplier—for now. Regardless of what the reason, it is important for you to remember that things will change again. While they may not be in the market for your product or service right now, times and needs and circumstances will change. When they do, you want to be the vendor or solution that is top of mind for them.

Because there is nothing more frustrating than calling your prospect back after six months only to find that they just signed on with your competition, you need to find an effective and reliable way to be in front of them and thereby remain top of mind. The best way I've found to do this is to use an automatic card system that regularly sends your prospects a pre-written, beautiful card at pre-appointed intervals that you choose in advance. And to do this, I have used Send Out Cards (SOC) for years now.

I know I have mentioned this system in previous sections, but I want to go over it just a bit more in depth here as it is a powerful strategy for winning long-term business. The way it works is simplicity itself. For my top of mind program, what I have done is written eleven cards in advance and put them into an automatic prospecting campaign. Any time a prospect doesn't buy, I immediately put them into this campaign. As soon as I add their name, the system automatically sends them the first card in the campaign, and then each month after that, the system sends them the next card. Once I add a prospect or client's name in my database, I know that they are going to receive a physical greeting card for as long as the next 11 months! How is that for keeping top of mind?

This kind of card drip-marketing system has made me hundreds of thousands of dollars in business that I would not have gotten otherwise. Because I know that things do change, and that my prospects will need my services sooner or later, I can be assured that when they do need sales training or script writing or coaching, I will be the solution they think of first. In fact, I have even gotten big deals from people I have never even spoken with before! Every now and then, I get phone calls from someone who was recommended by one of my prospects who has been receiving cards from me. The point is, physical greeting cards work. They are a unique way to stay in front of your prospect and a way to completely differentiate yourself from the many other vendors and salespeople who are just sending emails that get deleted.

The other cool thing about SOC is that you can completely customize your cards by easily making them using your own graphics or photographs or by scanning in your business card, and much more. One of my favorite things to do is to take a picture of my prospect if we have met in person and then upload that image to a card I send to them. Believe me, they don't throw those cards away! Also, SOC has over 18,000 high-quality cards to choose from that are already formatted and written. You can choose cards from a hundred different categories for as many occasions as you can think of!

While the campaign function is the one I use the most, you can also send birthday cards, congratulations cards, and a full array of gifts as well. Want to make a really big impression? Why not send your favorite clients a birthday card and a four-pack of delicious brownies on their birthday? You can do all that affordably and easily with a click of a mouse.

Speaking of affordability, the cost of sending out a beautiful, customized card is less than $1.50. And that includes postage! (SOC even puts a real postage stamp on the envelope.) Compare that to cards you find in stores, as well as all the time and energy you spend driving there and browsing the card aisles, and so on. SOC makes staying in front of your prospects (and customers) easy, fun, and highly effective. By the way, I also use SOC in my personal life as well, sending customized cards of our family's vacations, and using it to send birthday cards and gifts, and special cards for special occasions. It's great fun.

By the way, using SOC is easy to do and they give you many ways to use their service. You can use it one card at a time, or you can choose to save a bit of money by using their service monthly, and so forth. You can even make money with SOC by signing up as a distributor and then introducing others to the service as well. Some people, in fact, have decided to make SOC their primary business and many of their distributors make thousands of dollars in recurring revenue each month because of the downline they have created. How you use SOC—and for what purpose—is completely up to you.

Again, I use SOC as a strong, "top of mind" follow-up system for my prospects and customers, and it puts me way ahead of my competition and earns me deals regularly. It can do the same for you, too. If you haven't done so already, then visit: www.sendoutcards/mrinsidesales to see how easy this system is and to browse their card catalogue. You can even send a card to yourself to try out the system and test the quality of them on me! (Just visit the link given here to try it.) Whatever your interest level is, I highly recommend you explore sending cards if you want to begin winning more deals from prospects who are going to be in need of your product or service at some point in the future. Remember, *you* want to be the person they call when things change.

CONCLUSION

Whew! We have covered a lot of proven techniques that will change the way you sell over the phone. Are you excited? You should be! By now you are probably thinking that these word-for-word scripts and selling strategies are better than what you have been ad-libbing on your own. By now, you should be chomping at the bit to get out there and try some of these techniques.

Good for you!

Let me warn you what your biggest challenge is going to be: overcoming your old, ineffective, habitual way of doing things. If you are not careful, you will automatically default to your old ways of reacting and responding—your old habits. You will just naturally stop trying to use these new and more effective responses, and before long, this book will be in the bottom drawer along with all the other books on sales you have bought.

This is why it is important to go back to the 10 characteristics of top sales performers and commit to implementing these in your sales routine. Commit to adapting and using these new word-for-word scripts until *they* become your new habit. As someone once said: "First we form habits. Then they form us." By committing to learning these new core sales skills, you will get better, day after day, and your automatic way of handling sales situations will become stronger and you will begin winning more sales.

Make a commitment to recording yourself for 90 days so you can catch yourself using your old habits and then correct yourself and your technique. After you have adapted these scripts to your product or service and your personality, record them into your smartphone and commit to listening to yourself recite them 30 to 40 times. If you do, then just like you know the words to your favorite song, you will memorize them and be able to use them just when you need them. They will become your automatic responses, and suddenly you will find that you have the freedom to actually listen to what your prospect is saying. This is when you achieve true mastery over sales. It is a skill that you can develop, and it becomes a gift that keeps giving to you for years to come.

Let me end with a true story that happened a few short years ago. I was on my way to meet with a new consulting prospect, a business owner of a tech firm in Santa Monica, California. I got into my Mercedes and drove to the local Starbucks to get a venti drip for the drive. As I stood in line, I glanced over my shoulder at the corner of Topanga and Ventura Boulevard, and I saw the RTD bus pull up and let passengers off. One guy started to make his way toward Starbucks, and there was something vaguely familiar about the way he walked. He had a very pronounced up-and-down motion as the heel of each foot leapt off the ground before the front of his foot lifted up.

As he entered the store, there was something familiar about his face as well. It was suddenly my turn to order, which I did, and as I got my drink and moved past the line, he broke into a big smile as I passed and said, "Mike Brooks!" I admitted I was, and he told me his name was John, and that we used to work together all those years ago at the investment house we were both employed with at the time. I moved over to get my half tablespoon of sugar, and then he joined me at the coffee bar.

He asked how I was doing, and I told him great. I filled him in on my consulting, speaking, and publishing career, and how I was flying all over the country teaching sales teams word-for-word scripted techniques on how to sell more. He listened, vaguely, and then I asked him how he was doing.

He told me that he was on his way to apply for a new job in the same investment industry, and he gave me a discouraged look of knowing as he said this. He said things were tough, but that he was hoping this company would be the one. He mentioned that scripts had never worked for him, and that he always found that he needed to "go with the flow" of the conversation. I briefly thought of trying to convince him differently, but instead just gave him my card and told him that if I could help in any way, he should reach back out to me. He took it, and we walked outside. He turned toward the next bus stop, and I headed over to my Mercedes. I never heard from him.

As I got on the freeway, I thought back to when we used to work together. I remembered how we were both struggling while trying to sell investments. I also remembered what happened next. The company we worked for got a new sales manager who was a big believer in using phone scripts. He constructed a book of scripts and the company held a competition on who could close the most amount of new clients in a month using the word-for-word scripts. Needless to say, both John and I were skeptical.

There was one guy, however, who wasn't skeptical and who bought in to everything the new sales manager was saying. His name was Marty. Marty made it a point to read the scripts, word-for-word, on every call. When he got to the end of his presentation, I can still see him reading the scripted close and asking for the money. When the prospect said no, he would raise his eyebrows in that bored way and make a face as he moved on to the next rebuttal that usually began with, "I understand, _____, but there is something more important here." Then he would get to the end of that close and ask for the deal again.

Once more the prospect would say no and Marty faked a yawn, turned the pages of the script book and moved on to close number three. Then close numbers four and five. After about five closes and asking for the sale, something began to happen. The prospect started asking questions, and Marty would dutifully move on to another part of the script book and answer those questions. Invariably, each scripted answer would end with a tie-down like, "Did I answer that for you?" or "Does that make sense?" And if he got a "yes," Marty would ask for the sale again. "Then let's get you started," he would say.

After two or three more closes like this (if you have been count-ing, you will see that Marty would have asked for the sale anywhere from five to eight times by now), something magical would happen. The prospect would buy! Marty would beam as he began to take the prospect into the closing documents and cement the sale. Everyone sitting near Marty would watch this happen over and over again. I remember looking at John and seeing him shake his head in disbelief. I remember thinking that Marty was on to something.

At the end of that month, the new client contest ended. Marty won by a landslide. The average new accounts in the office had been between five and seven a month. Marty blew that out of the water by getting 22 new clients that month! To this day, I can see Marty shaking his head, raising his eyebrows, and turning to the next close in his script book. And I remember the look on his face as he received the check for $1,000 for winning the contest.

The reason I tell you this story is that I remember that experience made a believer out of me. Soon I, too, was reading the scripts, faking yawns, and turning to the next close. I was the one reading the scripts word-for-word and asking for the deal repeatedly, and soon I was the one receiving a check for closer of the month.

And John? Well, I still remember his resistance to using scripts. "They make you sound fake. I need to be able to go with the flow, man." John never did buy into the effectiveness of using proven scripts, and he didn't succeed at that company either. John was soon gone and moved on to greener pastures, where he undoubtedly still insisted on ad-libbing his responses and his sales career. And now, 15 years later, he was still looking for a new job where things might be better. Do you think there is a connection here?

As a parting piece of advice, I just want to encourage you to adopt and use the mantra, "If they (the other top producers in your company or industry) can do it, I can do it better." And I know you can. And, deep down, you know it, too. I encourage you to make this one-time commitment to yourself, your future, and your family to upgrade your core selling skills today. Over the coming year—and for many, many years to come—you will be eternally grateful you did. You will have a quality of life beyond your imagination, and you will suddenly find yourself doing and having the things that the majority of sales reps are never able to do or enjoy. One year from now, it could mean the difference between taking a city bus to find a new job or driving the car of your choice to a company that gives you ultimate fulfillment. The small price for that kind of life change—investing 90 days of your life in mastering these techniques—is a small price to pay for all that you will gain.

I should know. It happened to me, and it can happen to you as well. Believe in yourself, and get started today.

ACKNOWLEDGMENTS

No writer, and no sales professional, works alone. Success in every venture is achieved through the teamwork, the contributions, and the dedicated work of countless others. It would be impossible for me to thank all those who helped me bring this book to you, so I will name just a few of the people I owe so much to. If I don't mention you by name, just know that I am deeply grateful for everyone who helped me with this book, and you know who you are.

I would first like to acknowledge and thank my wife, Qi, for the tireless work she did, week after week, in proofing and offering invaluable suggestions on each and every section of this book. Thank you, honey, for the countless hours of patience, love, and encouragement you gave and continue to give to me. This book is the result of your effort as much as it is mine.

Next, I'd like to thank those sales professionals and motivators in the industry who were so important in my development as a budding sales producer. First, I'd like to thank my brother, Peter Brooks, who taught me some of the most fundamental and essential skills that I still use today. Two that I continually remind myself are: "Everybody you speak with is a person just like you. Treat them with respect." And, "You never know what the next phone call can bring—keep dialing, and you will run into amazing success." You were right in both instances—thank you, brother. I'd also like to thank the late (and great) Stan Billue. He truly was Mr. Fantastic! Also, I learned some of the most important motivational lessons from Bob Moawad, of the Edge Learning Institute. The practical tools of goal setting, positive affirmations, and the proper and purposeful use of your imagination have changed my life—and continue to do so.

I'd also like to acknowledge some of the people who took the time to review the manuscript copy of this book and offer their endorsement. I'd first like to thank Jeb Blount of Sales Gravy for writing the foreword to this book. Jeb, I know how busy your life is these days.

You've worked hard at becoming one of the top motivational sales leaders and speakers in the industry. I truly appreciate you taking time to help me with this book. I'd also like to thank Michael Krause for sharing his experience with publishing a book through a top publishing house, and for sharing his tips for the process. I'd like to thank Bruce Adorian, owner of the State Farm Agency here in Cary, North Carolina, for his review and endorsement of this book. Bruce, you are not only a caring and compassionate insurance professional, you've become a good friend and trusted business colleague as well. I value our mornings at Starbucks! And last, I'd like to thank Jeffrey Gitomer for his frequent support and for the knowledge and experience he has always shared with me so freely. It was Jeffrey's suggestion to call Matt Holt at John Wiley & Sons, and that led directly to the published copy you are holding right now.

I'd further like to thank the team at Wiley for the wonderful experience I have had from the beginning to the end. I wish here to acknowledge Matt Holt for immediately believing in this book and for his support in getting it published. And I'd like to thank Liz Gildea, my editor and chief advocate, for her belief in me and my material. There are many others at Wiley to whom I owe many thanks, and I want you all to know that I couldn't have done this without you. Thank you!

And finally, I want to thank you, the reader, for investing your time, your money, and your belief that this book, and its contents, can make a difference in your sales career and in your life. I have sat at desks just like yours and made the same kinds of calls you have made, and I want you to know that I have the utmost respect for you and what you do each and every day. I hope that one day our paths cross and that I'm able to offer something more to help you achieve the goals and the dreams that got you into the sales industry to begin with. I truly wish you all the success you work so hard for.

CONNECT WITH MIKE BROOKS

CALL ME

If you or your team needs help prospecting, setting appointments, or closing sales over the phone, then reach out to me. I'll be happy to take time to discuss your specific situation and offer some suggestions and resources that can boost your production right away.

How to reach me: When I'm not onsite training at a client's location, or speaking at sales conventions or delivering keynotes, then I'm in my office working with clients by phone. You can call me directly here: (919) 267-4202. Also, like you, I'm looking at my email all the time, so you can email me here: Mike@MrInsideSales.com. Additionally, you should visit my website and take advantage of the additional resources I offer, like subscribing to my free weekly e-zine, *The Secrets of the Top 20 Percent*, or the wealth of information on my inside sales blog. My website is: www.mrinsidesales.com.

OTHER RESOURCES THAT WILL HELP YOU

Onsite Training: Nothing is more impactful for your company or your team than to have me onsite to present a customized inside sales training at your location. I take the time to learn about your unique product and sale, and then I customize scripts and solutions that your team can begin using on their next phone call to reach more prospects and close more sales.

Keynotes and Speaking Engagements: If you are in need of a dynamic and proven speaker who delivers not only motivational energy, but proven, word-for-word techniques that your team can use the moment they get back to the office to make a real difference, then contact our office today. I customize all my keynotes and breakout sessions by interviewing you and your top sales producers. Then I give all your team members the practical, real-world techniques that work in your sales environment. I am booked months in advance, so the more notice the better to secure me as your next—and best—speaker.

Management Training: How much training have you given the most important person on your sales team? Most inside sales managers were promoted because they were great producers, but they have rarely been given the tools, skills, and training they need to be great leaders. My half-day management training will give them the specific tools they need to mentor, measure, and motivate your team.

One-on-One Coaching: If you are a business owner who needs to grow your inside sales team—and get them to hit or exceed their monthly revenue numbers—then let me show you how. For over 30 years, I've been helping companies define a winning sales process, create an effective sales script playbook, and develop a proven sales model that you can use to scale and grow your company. Call me to find out how.

On-Demand Sales Training Programs: Training your sales team, and teaching them now to succeed in the selling situations they run into every day, is *the most important thing* you can do to have a successful team and successful company. I offer on-demand programs your team can use over and over again to learn and adopt these powerful skills. I also create customized, on-demand, sales training programs for companies that you can use over and over again to grow and scale a multimillion-dollar inside sales team. Ask me how.

Products to Help You and Your Sales Team Sell More: If you liked this book, then you'll love my other products. Whether you are looking for my original book of scripts, *The Ultimate Book of Phone Scripts*, or my five-CD series, "*How to Double Your Income Selling Over the Phone,*" you will find these and many other products on my website.

Remember, every investment you make in yourself and your sales team pays for itself, month after month.

About the Author

Mike Brooks, Mr. Inside Sales

Mike Brooks is a master phone script writer and author of the best-selling book *The Ultimate Book of Phone Scripts*. That book has been endorsed by Bob Perkins, the founder and chairman of the American Association of Inside Sales Professionals (AA-ISP). For more than 30 years, Mike has been recognized as *the* authority on inside sales training and phone script development. He is a highly sought out speaker at inside sales conferences and sales conventions, and has also been voted one of the most influential inside sales professionals by the AA-ISP for seven years running.

Mike started his career in the financial and securities industry and quickly became the top producer out of five branch offices in Southern California. Promoted to executive vice president of sales, he developed a Top 20 Percent Inside Sales Training Program that doubled corporate sales of private placements from 27 million to more than 58 million in his first year, and then more than doubled that again the next year—total revenue of more than $119 million. Mike then served as a VP of sales for other securities firms before starting his own consulting company, and is known throughout all industries as "Mr. Inside Sales."

Mike is hired by businesses, selling into both B-to-B and B-to-C verticals, to develop and implement proven sales processes, and develop customized script playbooks that help companies immediately scale and grow multimillion-dollar inside sales teams. He also offers customized sales training programs, works as a virtual VP of sales, and offers executive coaching programs to business owners and top sales professionals around the world. For more information, visit his website: mrinsidesales.com.

INDEX